Camera Networks

The Acquisition and Analysis of Videos over Wide Areas

Synthesis Lectures on Computer Vision

Editors
Gérard Medioni, *University of Southern California*
Sven Dickinson, *University of Toronto*

Synthesis Lectures on Computer Vision is edited by Gérard Medioni of the University of Southern California and Sven Dickinson of the University of Toronto. The series will publish 50-to 150 page publications on topics pertaining to computer vision and pattern recognition. The scope will largely follow the purview of premier computer science conferences, such as ICCV, CVPR, and ECCV. Potential topics include, but not are limited to:

- Applications and Case Studies for Computer Vision

- Color, Illumination, and Texture

- Computational Photography and Video

- Early and Biologically-inspired Vision

- Face and Gesture Analysis

- Illumination and Reflectance Modeling

- Image-Based Modeling

- Image and Video Retrieval

- Medical Image Analysis

- Motion and Tracking

- Object Detection, Recognition, and Categorization

- Segmentation and Grouping

- Sensors

- Shape-from-X

- Stereo and Structure from Motion

- Shape Representation and Matching

- Statistical Methods and Learning

- Performance Evaluation

- Video Analysis and Event Recognition

Camera Networks: The Acquisition and Analysis of Videos over Wide Areas
Amit K. Roy-Chowdhury and Bi Song

ISBN: 978-3-031-00683-8   paperback
ISBN: 978-3-031-01811-4   ebook

DOI 10.1007/978-3-031-01811-4

A Publication in the Springer series
SYNTHESIS LECTURES ON COMPUTER VISION

Lecture #4
Series Editors: Gérard Medioni, *University of Southern California*
                Sven Dickinson, *University of Toronto*
Series ISSN
Synthesis Lectures on Computer Vision
Print 2153-1056   Electronic 2153-1064

Camera Networks

The Acquisition and Analysis of Videos over Wide Areas

Amit K. Roy-Chowdhury and Bi Song
University of California, Riverside

SYNTHESIS LECTURES ON COMPUTER VISION #4

ABSTRACT

As networks of video cameras are installed in many applications like security and surveillance, environmental monitoring, disaster response, and assisted living facilities, among others, image understanding in camera networks is becoming an important area of research and technology development. There are many challenges that need to be addressed in the process. Some of them are listed below.
- Traditional computer vision challenges in tracking and recognition, robustness to pose, illumination, occlusion, clutter, recognition of objects, and activities;
- Aggregating local information for wide area scene understanding, like obtaining stable, long-term tracks of objects;
- Positioning of the cameras and dynamic control of pan-tilt-zoom (PTZ) cameras for optimal sensing;
- Distributed processing and scene analysis algorithms;
- Resource constraints imposed by different applications like security and surveillance, environmental monitoring, disaster response, assisted living facilities, etc.

In this book, we focus on the basic research problems in camera networks, review the current state-of-the-art and present a detailed description of some of the recently developed methodologies. The major underlying theme in all the work presented is to take a network-centric view whereby the overall decisions are made at the network level. This is sometimes achieved by accumulating all the data at a central server, while at other times by exchanging decisions made by individual cameras based on their locally sensed data.

Chapter 1 starts with an overview of the problems in camera networks and the major research directions. Some of the currently available experimental testbeds are also discussed here. One of the fundamental tasks in the analysis of dynamic scenes is to track objects. Since camera networks cover a large area, the systems need to be able to track over such wide areas where there could be both overlapping and non-overlapping fields of view of the cameras, as addressed in Chapter 2. Distributed processing is another challenge in camera networks and recent methods have shown how to do tracking, pose estimation and calibration in a distributed environment. Consensus algorithms that enable these tasks are described in Chapter 3. Chapter 4 summarizes a few approaches on object and activity recognition in both distributed and centralized camera network environments. All these methods have focused primarily on the analysis side given that images are being obtained by the cameras. Efficient utilization of such networks often calls for active sensing, whereby the acquisition and analysis phases are closely linked. We discuss this issue in detail in Chapter 5 and show how collaborative and opportunistic sensing in a camera network can be achieved. Finally, Chapter 6 concludes the book by highlighting the major directions for future research.

KEYWORDS

wide area tracking, distributed video analysis, Kalman consensus, distributed tracking, recognition, active sensing, opportunistic sensing

Amit: To my parents for all they have done

Bi: To my parents

Contents

Preface

Camera networks is a highly interdisciplinary area of research that has been very active over the last few years. In this book, we focus specifically on the topic of video understanding in camera networks and touch upon the other related areas (e.g., communication resources, machine learning, cooperative control of multi-agent systems) as they pertain to this main focus. Our goal is to provide an overview of the current state-of-the-art in one single document. Researchers interested in the broad area or a particular sub-topic can start out with this book and then move on to specific papers that provide more details.

We divide the area of video analysis in camera networks along the lines of traditional computer vision – tracking, recognition, geometric calibration, 3D estimation, active vision. In each of these, we specifically focus on issues that are relevant to camera networks. For example, in tracking this entails analysis of handoff between non-overlapping cameras, while in active sensing, cooperative control of the camera network is addressed. An issue that is specific to camera networks is distributed processing and we dedicate a chapter to this aspect.

In writing this book, we build upon our experience in working on various research projects related to camera networks. We would like to thank the different funding agencies that made this possible: National Science Foundation through grants ECS-0622176 and CNS-0551741, Office of Naval Research through N00014-09-1-0666 and N00014-09-C-0388, Army Research Office through W911NF-07-1-0485, and CISCO Inc. The first author would like to thank his students and collaborators in this area who have contributed immensely to his understanding of the subject – his former student and co-author Dr. B. Song, without whom this book would never have been possible, his current students Mr. C. Ding and Mr. A. T. Kamal, and his colleagues Prof. B. Bhanu and Prof. J. A. Farrell, with whom he has shared some of the research projects. He is indebted to his advisor Prof. R. Chellappa (Univ. of Maryland, College Park) for initiating him into the world of academic research and to Prof. B. S. Manjunath (Univ. of California, Santa Barbara) for all the help and support in the initial years of his academic career.

Both of us are immensely grateful for the continuous support from our families – the joy they bring makes the whole effort worthwhile. We thank our parents for all that they have done and dedicate this book to them.

Amit K. Roy-Chowdhury and Bi Song
January 2012

C H A P T E R   1

An Introduction to Camera Networks

Networks of video cameras are being installed in many applications, like surveillance and security, disaster response, and environmental monitoring, among others. Currently, most of the data collected by such networks is analyzed manually, a task that is extremely tedious and reduces the potential of the installed networks. Therefore, it is essential to develop tools for automatically analyzing the data collected from these cameras and summarizing the results in a manner that is meaningful to the end user. This motivates the study of camera networks as a challenging research problem and a pressing social necessity. This book provides a comprehensive overview of the state-of-the-art video analysis using a camera network and identifies the main directions of future work.

1.1   RESEARCH DIRECTIONS

Major strides have been made in recent years in the area of sensor networks, which have a direct bearing on camera networks research. However, the unique characteristics of camera networks differentiate them from other types of sensor networks and introduce certain challenges. First of all, compared to most other sensors which provide 1D data signals as measurements, cameras provide 2D images as a function of time. The richer information content leads to higher complexity of data processing and analysis. Second, unlike other types of sensors which collect information in their vicinity, cameras are directional sensors and capture images of distant scenes from a certain direction. Neighboring cameras might collect information about very different parts of the same scene. Moreover, many image analysis algorithms in camera networks require information about the cameras' settings, such as locations and orientations, which need to be obtained through a camera calibration process.

Below are a few of the unique research directions that are associated with camera networks.

1.1.1   CAMERA NETWORK TOPOLOGY

Camera networks cover large areas. A fundamental task in wide-area surveillance is to monitor the flow of traffic in the area. This requires understanding the patterns of flow between cameras that are observing the area. When the cameras have non-overlapping field of views, there exist unobserved areas in the camera network. In this scenario, it is critical to understand where an object leaving the view of one camera is likely to appear next. The probability distribution that describes this likelihood is called the transition model. The network topology is represented as a graph, with camera as nodes and edges connecting adjacent cameras. Two cameras are adjacent if an object can travel between them without passing through any other cameras, i.e., a direct path exists between the two cameras. The transition model describes the probability of traffic moving along each path and the time it takes to travel along that path (this can also be represented as a distribution). The camera network topology learning problem is usually referred to as estimating both network topology and transition model, either during a separate training phase or continuously during operation.

Based on whether or not different cameras in the network have overlaps in their fields of view, the topology learning problem can be divided into two types: non-overlapping and overlapping. Much of the work in this area considers cameras with non-overlapping fields of view. Mutual information was used in [Tieu et al., 2005] as a measure of statistical dependence to infer the camera network topology, and a Monte Carlo Markov Chain was using for sampling correspondences between observations. To exploit the abundant visual information provided by the imaging sensors, an appearance-integrated cross-correlation model was proposed in [Niu and Grimson, 2006] for topology inference on vehicle tracking data, and person identities were integrated with appearance in [Zou et al., 2009]. Ground-truth trajectory and object appearance information was used in [Javed et al., 2003] to learn the topology of a set of cameras as well as the pairwise illumination change between cameras during a training phase. A Bayesian approach was described in [Farrell et al., 2007] for learning higher-order transition models, i.e., where moving objects will probably go after they pass through one or more cameras. In [Farrell and Davis, 2008], a decentralized approach was proposed for camera network topology discovery based on sequential Bayesian estimation using a modified multinomial distribution. In [Markis et al., 2004], cross correlation and covariance over thousands of observations of departure and arrival times were utilized to identify adjacent cameras. This method also works for overlapping cameras, as negative transition time indicates that objects enter one camera's view before leaving another camera.

To infer the topology of camera networks with overlapping field of views, a Sequential Probability Ratio Test (SPRT) was utilized to accept or reject the possibility that two cameras observe the same scene based on accumulated sequential detections [Mandel et al., 2007]. A method for inferring which cameras in the network have overlapping fields of view was presented in [Cheng et al., 2007] based on a fixed-length message of automatically detected key points that each camera broadcasts to the rest of the network; the message is called "feature digest" which is a compressed representation of a camera's detected features.

1.1.2   WIDE AREA TRACKING

Object tracking is one of the most fundamental tasks for higher-level automated video content analysis. The tracking problem can be defined as estimating trajectories of moving objects over time. In addition to challenges in tracking a single object, like occlusion, appearance variation, and image noise, the critical issue in multi-target tracking is data association, i.e., the problem of linking a sequence of observations across image frames based on the fact that they belong to the same object.

This is critical in camera networks because it is very likely that many objects will be in the scene simultaneously and they will move between cameras. Also, it is necessary to track over long time intervals when considering wide area scene analysis. Although a large number of trackers exist, their reliability falls off quickly with the length of the tracks. Stable, long-term tracking is still a challenging problem. Moreover, for multiple targets, we have to consider the interaction between the targets which may cause errors like switching between tracks, missed detections and false detections. In addition, wide area tracking over a camera network requires solving the problem of handoff between cameras, which makes it more difficult to construct correspondences across camera views due to significant lighting and view changes.

To track multiple objects, a lot of effort has been devoted to solving the data association problem based on the results of object detection. Multi-Hypothesis Tracking (MHT) in [Reid, 1979] and Joint Probabilistic Data Association Filters (JPDAF) in [Bar-Shalom and Fortmann, 1988] are two representative methods. In order to overcome the large computational cost of MHT and JPDAF, various optimization algorithms such as Linear Programming [Jiang et al., 2007], Quadratic Boolean Programming [Leibe et al., 2007], and Hungarian algorithm [Perera et al., 2006] are used for data association. In [Yu et al., 2007], data association was achieved through a MCMC sampling-based framework.

Some of the existing methods on tracking in a camera network include [Huang and Russel, 1997], [Javed et al., 2003] and [Kettnaker and Zabih, 1999]. In [Huang and Russel, 1997], a probabilistic approach was presented for finding corresponding vehicles across cameras on a highway. The appearance of vehicles was modeled by the mean of the color and transition times were modeled as Gaussian distributions. A graph-theoretic framework for addressing the problem of tracking in a network of cameras was proposed in [Javed et al., 2003]. A Bayesian formulation of the problem of reconstructing the path of objects across multiple non-overlapping cameras was described in [Kettnaker and Zabih, 1999] using color histograms for object appearance. The authors in [Rahimi and Darrell, 2004] used location and velocity of objects moving across multiple non-overlapping cameras to estimate the calibration parameters of the cameras and the target's trajectory. In [Leoputra et al., 2006], a particle filter was used to switch between track prediction for non-overlapping cameras and tracking within a camera. In [Kang et al., 2004], the authors presented a method for tracking in overlapping stationary and pan-tilt-zoom cameras by maximizing a joint motion and appearance probability model. In [Song and Roy-Chowdhury, 2007, 2008], a multi-objective optimization framework was presented for tracking in a camera network. In Chapter 2, we will present details on some methods that address different aspects of tracking in a camera network.

1.1.3 DISTRIBUTED PROCESSING

In many applications, it is desirable that the video analysis tasks be decentralized. For example, there may be bandwidth constraints (e.g., mobile networks), security issues, and difficulty in analyzing a huge amount of data centrally. Distributed systems can also be easily installed and allow for operations in remote and hostile environments, possibly alongside humans. They can provide very valuable initial inputs to humans (e.g., search and rescue personnel) keeping them out of harms way and enabling operations in wider variety of environments than currently feasible. In such situations, the cameras would have to act as autonomous agents making decisions in a decentralized manner. At the same time, however, the decisions of the cameras need to be coordinated so that there is a consensus about the task. In a distributed camera network, each camera node processes its own image data locally, extracts relevant information and collaborates with other cameras reach a shared, global analysis of the scene.

Although there are a number of methods in video analysis that deal with multiple cameras, *distributed* processing in camera networks has received much less attention. For example, some of the well-known methods for learning a network topology [Markis et al., 2004, Tieu et al., 2005], tracking over the network [Rahimi and Darrell, 2004, Song and Roy-Chowdhury, 2007], object/behavior detection, matching across cameras, and camera handoff and camera placement [Alahi et al., 2008, Ermis et al., 2008, Javed et al., 2000, Stancil et al., 2008, Zhao et al., 2008] do not address the issue of distributed processing. In [Medeiros et al., 2008], a cluster-based Kalman filter was proposed for decentralized tracking, where a camera is selected as a cluster head and aggregates information in the cluster. In [Qureshi and Terzopoulos, 2007], a mixture between a distributed and a centralized tracking scheme was presented which uses both static and PTZ cameras in a virtual camera network environment.

Recently, some problems in video analysis have been addressed in a distributed manner. A distributed algorithm for the calibration of a camera network was presented in [Devarajan et al., 2008a]. The problems of object detection, tracking, recognition and pose estimation in distributed camera networks were considered in [Sankaranarayanan et al., 2008, Wu and Aghajan, 2008].

Distributed processing has been extensively studied in the multi-agent systems and cooperative control literature [Olfati-Saber et al., 2007]. Consensus-based approaches have been especially popular. In a network of agents, consensus can be defined as reaching an agreement through cooperation regarding a certain quantity of interest that depends on the measurement information available from all agents. Methods have been developed for reaching consensus on a state observed independently by multiple sensors. A theoretical framework for defining and solving consensus problems for networked dynamic systems was introduced in [Olfati-Saber and Murray, 2004]. Consensus algorithms for reaching an agreement without computing any objective function appeared in the work of [Jadbabaie et al., 2003]. Consensus schemes have also been gaining popularity in computer vision applications involving multiple cameras, such as pose estimation [Tron et al., 2008] and activity recognition [Song et al., 2010b]. Chapter 3 describes distributed processing algorithms in camera networks in detail.

1.1.4   CAMERA NETWORK CONTROL (ACTIVE VISION)

In many applications, the cameras have pan, tilt and zoom parameters that can be modified and it is necessary to develop strategies for this purpose. The network would then be capable of reconfiguring itself by modifying these parameters. One of the advantages of having a dynamically self-configurable network is that it could be prohibitively expensive to have a static setup that would cater to all possible situations. For example, suppose we needed to focus on one person (possibly non-cooperative) or specific features (e.g., face) of the person as he walks around in an area and obtain a high resolution image of him while keeping track of other activities also going on in the terminal. To achieve this, we will either need to dynamically change the parameters of the cameras where this person is visible or have a setup whereby it would be possible to capture high resolution imagery irrespective of where the person is in the area. The second option would be very expensive and a huge waste of resources, both technical and economical. Therefore, we need a way to control the cameras based on the sensed data. Currently, similar applications try to cover the entire area or the most important parts of it with a set of passive cameras, and have difficulty in acquiring high resolution shots selectively.

The issue of actively controlling the camera parameters is closely tied to camera placement since they both affect the quality of images that can be captured. Optimal camera placement strategies were proposed in [Zhao et al., 2008] and solved by using a camera placement metric that captures occlusion in 3-D environments. In [Erdem and Sclaroff, 2006], a solution to the problem of optimal camera placement given some coverage constraints was presented and can be used to come up with an initial camera configuration. Another relevant problem in camera control is to construct the mapping between the camera parameter space and a reference frame, which can be either an image plane or a ground plane. In [Davis, 2011], a method was proposed to map any pixel location in video image to its corresponding camera PTZ parameter. The authors also addressed a geo-registration technique to map the PTZ camera viewspaces to a wide-area aerial orthophotography (e.g., Google Map Image).

Some recent work has dealt with the problem of reconfiguring a camera network by changing the PTZ parameters of the individual cameras. The path planning inspired approach proposed by [Qureshi and Terzopoulos, 2009] used a mixed network of cameras. Static cameras were used to track all targets in a virtual environment while PTZ cameras were assigned to obtain high resolution video from the targets. A method for determining good sensor configurations that would maximize performance measures was introduced in [Mittal and Davis, 2008]. The configuration framework is based on the presence of random occluding objects and two techniques are proposed to analyze the visibility of the objects. A recent distributed approach in [Piciarelli et al., 2009] uses the Expectation-Maximization (EM) algorithm to find the optimal configuration of PTZ cameras given a map of activities. A framework for distributed control and target assignment in camera networks was presented in [Soto et al., 2009], in which cooperative network control ideas based on multi-player learning in games [Fudenberg and Levine, 1998] were used. In Chapter 5, the issue of camera network control is analyzed in detail.

1.1.5   MOBILE CAMERA NETWORKS

Consider an intelligent network of mobile agents, each equipped with visual sensors and the capability of analyzing its own data and taking decisions in coordination with other agents. This would enable the agents to maneuver themselves optimally so as to obtain images that can be analyzed with a high degree of reliability. We term such a network of agents as Mobile Camera Networks (MCNs). Designing such a system would require tightly integrating the sensing, navigation and camera control tasks to track, image and identify targets. They would have a high impact in applications like disaster management and operations in hostile territories, where it is not possible to set up an operating infrastructure beforehand.

Let us consider an example scenario where a number of mobile agents, each equipped with vision sensors, is released in a certain area with the mission of capturing frontal, high-resolution facial images of targets. We assume that the robots have limited communication capabilities between neighbors (i.e., they cannot exchange the video, but can exchange processed estimates like target locations), and that the processing is distributed over the network with no central server accumulating all the information. The overall mission objective can now be represented in terms of specific objectives for each agent. These would include the agents positioning themselves so that possible target locations are covered, detecting human targets and their faces, and estimating camera parameters and locations so as to obtain the facial shots. Note that for this entire process to happen, it is necessary to integrate the sensing, routing and scene analysis phases. The camera parameters and agent trajectories need to be optimized jointly so as to meet the scene understanding criteria.

The problem has similarities to the Vehicle Routing Problem (VRP) where a set of mobile agents coordinate between themselves for resource allocation, task assignment, communication or movement with the goal of servicing a set of tasks [Bullo et al., 2011, Zhang and Leonard, 2010]. A task is completed when a vehicle travels to the task location and provides the required services. Equipping these vehicles with cameras would enable tasks in which visual analysis is key, e.g., visual tracking and monitoring, object and event recognition. This would be achieved by opportunistically acquiring images that satisfy the application requirements. Moreover, it would enable the agents to navigate in dynamic, unknown and adversarial environments by coordinating with other agents, much like a group of humans can. The MCN problem, while having similarities to the VRP, has a few fundamental distinctions.

In the MCN problem, the exact location of where the vehicles need to go to achieve a specific goal may be unknown. Also, the optimal location needs to be decided in conjunction with the camera PTZ parameters and an understanding of the dynamic scene characteristics. As an example, consider that the agents have to take high resolution face shots of people moving around in an area. The targets are dynamic and their locations need to be estimated by the agents in real time by analyzing the sensed videos. This would require the vehicles, as a team, to be able to image all the probable target locations at each time instant, in addition to obtaining the high resolution shots. Therefore, the routing has to be decided based on satisfaction of multiple objectives (in this example, tracking all targets and taking high resolution shots), which will determine the locations of the agents and the camera PTZ parameters. This makes the control of mobile camera networks distinct from and more challenging than existing VRP solutions.

The MCN problem is a very interesting and challenging problem with clear practical applications. However, there are no existing solutions, except for some special cases [Quintero et al., 2010]. We will not deal with this problem further in this book and leave it to future researchers to come up with suitable solutions.

1.1.6 SIMULATION IN CAMERA NETWORKS

Camera networks lie at the intersection of Computer Vision and Sensor Networks. Researchers from both fields are interested in sensing and control issues that especially arise in the visual surveillance of large public spaces. However, deploying a large-scale physical surveillance system may not be easy for those who are interested in experimenting with multi-camera systems. As a means of overcoming this barrier, as well as to avoid privacy laws that restrict the monitoring of people in public spaces, the *Virtual Vision* paradigm was introduced in [Terzopoulos, 2003], which facilitates research through the virtual reality simulation of populated urban spaces with camera sensor networks. Within the virtual vision framework, a surveillance system comprising smart cameras that provide perceptive coverage of a virtual reconstruction of New York City's original Pennsylvania Station was developed [Terzopoulos and Qureshi, 2011]. This virtual train station is populated by autonomously self-animating virtual pedestrians; virtual passive and active cameras generate multiple synthetic video feeds that emulate those generated by real surveillance cameras monitoring public spaces.

Virtual vision has several advantages: The virtual cameras are very easily relocated and reconfigured, the ground-truth data of the virtual world is readily accessible, experiments are repeatable, and simulated camera networks can be actively controlled thus enabling performance analysis of different camera control algorithms.

1.1.7 EXPERIMENTAL TESTBEDS

Experimentation in camera networks can be very challenging for a number of reasons. First, a system consisting of a large number of cameras may not be accessible to researchers. Even when such a system is available, engineering issues like data transmission rates or processing capabilities may limit the kinds of experiments that may be conducted. Moreover, since camera networks span a wide area, it is hard to design controlled experiments that are also practically relevant. The complexity of real-world environments where camera networks are most likely to be deployed, like an airport or a shopping mall, are very hard to replicate in a research setting. Below we list some systems that are currently available and which can be used by researchers in their experimentation. This list is by no means complete; it is intended to provide a sampling of some of the existing camera network experimental testbeds.

In the early 2000s, a virtual world was developed at the University of Toronto to serve as a software laboratory for carrying out camera networks research. This involved a large-scale digital reproduction of the Penn train station complete with cameras and autonomous pedestrians [Terzopoulos, 2003]. The Sensorium at Boston University was built around the year 2003 and is composed of wireless cameras spread over multiple rooms [Ocean et al., 2006]. All the projects at the Sensorium have the common goal of merging the physical and cyber worlds allowing development of assisted environments for people with disabilities. An Outdoor Video Sensor Network Laboratory, composed of over 30 PTZ cameras, has been developed at U.C. Riverside. This system also has a number of indoor cameras, infra-red and 3D sensors, and ground and aerial unmanned vehicles. A wide-area video understanding dataset was collected in this environment and is available to researchers (Videoweb Activities Dataset) [Denina et al., 2011]. The cameras in this facility are connected over a wireless network allowing for research in resource-constrained and distributed environments. In 2009, researchers at U.C. Santa Barbara installed a large network of static and PTZ cameras in the hallways of all five floors of a campus building and at various other locations on campus. They were interested in many different applications ranging from the understanding the patterns of movements within a building to developing distributed control algorithms [Xu et al., 2010]. On the other side of the globe, in the Nullarbor Desert in Western Australia, researchers from the Imperial College of London, Ondrejov Observatory in the Czech Republic, and the Western Australian Museum, set up a network of cameras track and find new meteorites [Bland et al., 2009]. This shows the potential for application of camera networks in environmental monitoring of remote regions.

1.1.8   APPLICATION DOMAINS

Camera sensor networks have a wide range of applications. A few representative ones are described below.

- Security and Surveillance: Surveillance is one of the primary applications of camera networks, where hundreds or even thousands of cameras monitor large public areas, such as airports, subways, etc. Since cameras usually provide raw video streams, it is difficult to interpret simultaneous video feeds manually. Initial machine or automated analysis of the data is highly desirable, and in some cases necessary, to guide and focus the operator's attention. Also, interesting events are rare and the task can get very tedious. Thus, it is desirable to utilize intelligent methods for extracting information from image data and come up with a meaningful representation for the user.

- Environmental monitoring: Camera networks can be used to monitor inaccessible areas remotely over a long period of time. Often in this scenario, the cameras are combined with other types of sensors, such that the cameras are triggered only when an event is detected by other sensors used in the network.

- Smart environments: A smart environment is an area where different kinds of smart devices are continuously working together to aid humans in their daily activities [Cook and Das, 2005]. Multiple sensors serve as "eyes" of the smart environments to capture in real-time the changing characteristics of the user and the environment. Visual sensors are very important components of the sensor network for their capability of capturing information-rich data. Representative examples of smart environments are smart meeting rooms and smart homes.

1.2   ORGANIZATION OF THE BOOK

This book provides a comprehensive review of work done in the context of video analysis in a network of cameras.

Chapter 2 considers the wide area tracking problem. We start off with a review of current work in multi-target tracking. We briefly describe two basic stochastic tracking methods – the Kalman Filter and Particle Filter, as well as two representative data association methods – Multi-Hypothesis Tracking (MHT) and Joint Probabilistic Data Association Filters (JPDAF). We then describe in detail the multi-target tracking problem in a multi-camera scenario. We briefly introduce the literature on tracking in a camera network, and then describe a few recent approaches that address various aspects of this problem.

Chapter 3 looks at the issue of distributed processing in camera network. We first illustrate the necessity of distributed processing. We review the principles that have been proposed for distributed estimation, especially the well-known consensus approaches. Then we show how to solve some fundamental tasks in computer vision in a distributed manner based on these principles, specifically pose estimation, calibration and tracking.

Chapter 4 focuses on the issues in object and activity recognition in a network of cameras. We begin the description by discussing some methods in object recognition and then describe one that explicitly considers resource constraints. Thereafter, we describe two methods that address the issues in modeling and recognition of activities that evolve over wide areas and are viewed by a large number of cameras (both overlapping and non-overlapping). Finally, a framework for distributed recognition using the previously described consensus algorithms is described.

Chapter 5 investigates active sensing in a camera network. We review a few recent approaches that address this problem and then focus on achieving this in a distributed setup. The goal is to develop a distributed strategy for coordinated control that relies on local decision-making at the camera nodes, while being aligned with a suitable global criteria for scene analysis as specified by the user. We show how to formulate the multi-camera control problem in the setting of a multi-player potential game. Examples for several representative applications, like collaborative sensing and opportunistic sensing, are provided.

The book concludes by providing a vision for future research directions in camera networks in Chapter 6.

CHAPTER 2

Wide-Area Tracking

Tracking in video can be defined as a problem of locating a moving object (or multiple objects) over time based on observations of the object in the images. In other words, the objective of a tracker is to associate target objects in consecutive video frames so as to determine their identities and locations. Multiple object tracking is one of the most fundamental tasks for higher level automated video content analysis because of its wide application in human-computer interaction, security and surveillance, video communication and compression, augmented reality, traffic control, and video editing. Maintaining the stability of tracks on multiple targets in video over extended time periods and wide areas remains a challenging problem. Some of the most basic tracking methods include the Kalman filter, particle filter and mean shift tracker. However, by themselves, these methods are usually not able to track over extended space-time horizons.

In addition to challenges in tracking a single object, like occlusion, appearance variation, and image noise, the critical issue in multi-target tracking is data association, i.e., the problem of linking a sequence of object observations in the presence of other observations. Wide-area tracking over a camera network introduces certain challenges that are unique to this particular application scenario. The main new challenge in the problem of tracking across non-overlapping camera networks is to find the associations between targets observed in different camera views. This is often referred to as the handoff problem in camera networks.

In this chapter, we start off with a review of current work in multi-target tracking. We briefly describe two most basic stochastic tracking methods – the Kalman Filter and Particle Filter, as well as two representative data association methods – Multi-Hypothesis Tracking (MHT) and Joint Probabilistic Data Association Filters (JPDAF) methods. We then describe in detail the multi-target tracking problem in a camera network scenario. We briefly introduce the literature on tracking in a camera network, and then describe a few recent methods that address various aspects of this problem.

2.1 REVIEW OF MULTI-TARGET TRACKING APPROACHES

Here, we review the literature on multi-target tracking. We start by describing two of the most basic methods - the Kalman Filter [Kalman, 1960] and Particle filter [Isard and Blake, 1998]. They are stochastic methods and solve tracking problems by taking the measurement and model uncertainties into account during object state estimation. They have been extensively used in the vision community for tracking, but these methods are not sufficient for tracking multiple objects by themselves. In [Hue et al., 2002], particle filters were used to track multiple objects by incorporating probabilistic MHT [Reid, 1979] for data association. We describe the MHT [Reid, 1979] and JPDAF [Bar-Shalom and Fortmann, 1988] strategies for tracking multiple targets.

2.1.1   KALMAN FILTER-BASED TRACKER

Consider a linear dynamical system with the following time propagation and observation models for a moving object in the scene:

$$\mathbf{x}(t+1) = \mathbf{A}\mathbf{x}(t) + \mathbf{B}\mathbf{w}(t); \quad \mathbf{x}(0) \tag{2.1}$$
$$\mathbf{z}(t) = \mathbf{F}(t)\mathbf{x}(t) + \mathbf{v}(t), \tag{2.2}$$

where $\mathbf{x}$ is the state of the target, $\mathbf{w}(t)$ and $\mathbf{v}(t)$ are zero mean white Gaussian noise ($\mathbf{w}(t) \sim \mathcal{N}(0, \mathbf{Q})$, $\mathbf{v}(t) \sim \mathcal{N}(0, \mathbf{R})$) and $\mathbf{x}(0) \sim \mathcal{N}(\mathbf{x}_0, \mathbf{P}_0)$ is the initial state of the target. The Kalman filter is composed of two step - prediction and correction. The prediction step uses the state model to predict the new state of the variables:

$$\bar{\mathbf{P}}(t+1) = \mathbf{A}\mathbf{P}(t)\mathbf{A}^T + \mathbf{B}\mathbf{Q}\mathbf{B}^T,$$
$$\bar{\mathbf{x}}(t+1) = \mathbf{A}\hat{\mathbf{x}}(t). \tag{2.3}$$

The correction step uses the current observations $\mathbf{z}(t)$ to update the object's state:

$$\mathbf{K}(t+1) = \bar{\mathbf{P}}(t+1)\mathbf{F}^T (\mathbf{F}\bar{\mathbf{P}}(t+1)\mathbf{F}^T + \mathbf{R})^{-1}$$
$$\hat{\mathbf{x}}(t+1) = \bar{\mathbf{x}}(t+1) + \mathbf{K}(t+1)(\mathbf{z}(t+1) - \mathbf{F}\bar{\mathbf{x}}(t+1)),$$
$$\hat{\mathbf{P}}(t+1) = (\mathbf{I} - \mathbf{K}(t+1)\mathbf{F})\bar{\mathbf{P}}(t+1). \tag{2.4}$$

Extensions to this basic approach dealing with non-linear models in video applications can be found in [Welch and Bishop, 1995].

2.1.2   PARTICLE FILTER-BASED TRACKER

The particle filter is often used in tracking applications in video to deal with non-linear and/or non-Gaussian models [Arulampalam et al., 2002]. For video applications, it is usually combined with motion detection and background subtraction algorithms.

Moving objects are often initialized using motion detection. The background modeling algorithm in [Stauffer and Grimson, 1998] can be used for its adaptability to illumination change, and to learn the multimodal background through time. In addition, by observing that most targets are on a ground plane, the rough ground plane area can be estimated [Hoiem et al., 2005]. Based on the ground plane information, false alarms can be removed significantly. The target regions can then be represented by rectangles with the state vector $X_t = [x, y, \dot{x}, \dot{y}, l_x, l_y]$, where (x, y) and $(\dot{x}, \dot{y})$ are the position and velocity of a target in the x and y directions respectively, and (l_x, l_y) denote the size of the rectangle.

The observation process is defined by the likelihood distribution, $p(I_t|X_t)$, where X_t is the state vector and I_t is the image observation at t. The observation models can be generated in many ways. Here, we provide an example by combining an appearance and a foreground response model, i.e.,

$$p(I_t|X_t) = p(I_t^a, I_t^f|X_t), \tag{2.5}$$

where I_t^a is the appearance information of I_t and I_t^f is the foreground response of I_t using a learned background model. I_t^f is a binary image with "1" for foreground and "0" for background. It is reasonable to assume that I_t^a and I_t^f are independent and thus (2.5) becomes

$$p(I_t|X_t) = p(I_t^a|X_t)p(I_t^f|X_t).$$

The appearance observation likelihood can be defined as

$$p(I_t^a|X_t) \propto \exp\{-B(ch(X_t), ch_0)^2\},$$

where $ch(X_t)$ is the color histogram associated with the rectangle region of X_t and ch_0 is color histogram of the initialized target. $B(.)$ is the Bhattachayya distance between two color histograms. The foreground response observation likelihood can be defined as

$$p(I_t^f|X_t) \propto \exp\left\{-\left(1 - \frac{\#F(X_t)}{\#X_t}\right)^2\right\},$$

where $\#F(X_t)$ is the number of foreground pixels in the rectangular region of X_t and $\#X_t$ is the total number of pixels in that rectangle. $\frac{\#F(X_t)}{\#X_t}$ represents the percentage of the foreground in that rectangle. The observation likelihood would be higher if more pixels in the rectangular region of X_t belong to the foreground. The reader should note that these are representative examples only. Various models are possible, and indeed, have been used in the literature.

The particle filter (PF) is a sequential Monte Carlo method (sequential importance sampling plus resampling) which provides at each t, an N sample Monte Carlo approximation to the prediction distribution, $\pi_{t|t-1}(dx) = Pr(X_t \in dx|I_{1:t-1})$, which is used to search for newly observed targets. These are then used to update $\pi_{t|t-1}$ to get the filtering (posterior) distribution, $\pi_{t|t}(dx) = P(X_t \in dx|I_{1:t})$. A particle filter is often used because the system and observation models are nonlinear and the posterior can temporarily become multi-model due to background clutter.

2.1.3 MULTI-HYPOTHESIS TRACKING (MHT)

This algorithm allows multiple hypotheses to be propagated in time as data is received. Multi-Hypothesis Tracking (MHT) is an iterative algorithm and is initialized with a set of current track hypotheses. Each hypothesis is a collection of disjoint tracks. For each hypothesis, the position of each object at the next time step is predicted. On receiving new data, each hypothesis is expanded into a set of new hypotheses by considering all measurement-to-track assignments for the tracks within the hypotheses. The probability of each new hypothesis is calculated. Often, for reasons of finite computer memory and computational power, the most unlikely hypotheses are deleted. The final tracks of the objects are the most likely set of associations over the time period. Note that MHT exhaustively enumerates all possible associations and is computationally exponential both in memory and time.

2.1.4 JOINT PROBABILISTIC DATA ASSOCIATION FILTERS (JPDAF)

This method is specifically designed for cluttered measurement models. The idea of Joint Probabilistic Data Association Filters (JPDAF) is to compute an expected state estimate over the various possibilities of measurement-to-track associations. Assuming we have n tracks and m measurements at time t, $Z(t) = \{z_1(t), \ldots, z_m(t)\}$, the state estimation of target i is

$$\hat{x}_i(t) = E[x_i(t)|Z(t)] = \sum_{j=1}^{m} E[x_i(t)|\chi_{ij}^t, Z(t)] P(\chi_{ij}^t|Z(t))$$

where χ_{ij} denotes the event that measurement j associates to target i.

In order to overcome the large computational cost of MHT and JPDAF, various optimization algorithms such as Linear Programming [Jiang et al., 2007], Quadratic Boolean Programming [Leibe et al., 2007], and Hungarian algorithm [Perera et al., 2006] are used for data association. In [Yu et al., 2007], data association was achieved through a MCMC sampling based framework. In [Shafique and Shah, 2005], a multiframe approach was proposed to preserve temporal coherency of speed and position. They formulated the correspondence as a graph theoretic problem for finding the best path for each point across multiple frames. They used a window of frames during point correspondence to handle occlusions whose durations are shorter than the temporal window used to perform matching.

2.2 TRACKING IN A CAMERA NETWORK - PROBLEM FORMULATION

We can think of tracking over a camera network as being equivalent to finding the associations between the tracklets obtained in different single cameras. Then, the problem boils down to finding the affinities between the tracklets so as to have tracks across cameras. Depending on the applications, various features can be used like appearance, motion, calibration, travel time, 3D models, etc. As an example, we show how the travel time between entry/exit nodes of different cameras can be used in the affinity modeling. The affinity between two tracks T_i^m and T_j^n that are observed at cameras C_m and C_n, respectively, can be estimated as the product of the similarity in appearance features and the travel time based similarity value, i.e.,

$$A(T_i^m, T_j^n) = A_a(T_i^m, T_j^n) A_\tau(T_i^m, T_j^n), \tag{2.6}$$

where $A_a(.)$ is the appearance affinity model and $A_\tau(.)$ represents the transition pattern between two camera nodes [Javed et al., 2003].

Our problem is to track P targets observed over a network of $C_1, ..., C_K$ cameras. This is abstracted as tracking over a collection of nodes, where each node is an entry or exit zone [Markis et al., 2004, Niu and Grimson, 2006] (these are usually small image regions). We assume that we know which camera each node can be viewed from (also referred to as a node belonging to a camera). Mathematically, each node is represented as n_i^c, where the subscript is a node index and the superscript represents the camera it belongs to. When we mention local processing at each node, we mean local computations at the camera to which that node belongs. For the purposes of this chapter, we assume that we can track people within the view of each camera. The cameras are synchronized and thus, each observation can be given a unique time stamp and location information in terms of the node it is observed from.

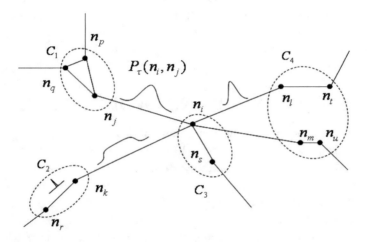

Figure 2.1: An example of a camera network; node n_i is linked to nodes (n_j, n_k, n_l, n_m) and a distribution of the travel time between them is known. (From [Song and Roy-Chowdhury, 2008])

A network architecture linking the nodes is known and can be computed from [Markis et al., 2004, Niu and Grimson, 2006]. By this we mean that given any pair of nodes $(n_i^c, n_j^d), i \neq j$, we have a link variable $l_{ij} = \{0, 1\}$, where 0 indicates that the two nodes are not linked, i.e., it is not possible to travel between those two nodes without traversing some other node, and 1 indicates that it is possible to travel between these two nodes directly. However, $l_{ij} = 1$ on a link does not rule out the possibility that a person could have travelled from n_i to n_j through some other node $n_k, k \neq i, j$. Besides this link variable, we also know a distribution of the travel time between two nodes belonging to different cameras, i.e., $P_\tau(n_i^c, n_j^d), i \neq j, c \neq d$, where $P : \Re^+ \to [0, 1]$. One of these nodes must be an entry node and the other an exit node. Travel time distribution between nodes belonging to the same camera are not needed, as they can be viewed completely and transitions between them tracked in the image plane.

Observations at each node are represented as feature vectors $\mathbf{F}_{n,t}$, where n indicates the node it is observed at and t the time of observation. Each node (i.e., the camera the node belongs to) receives information about the feature vectors from all other nodes that it is linked to. Making this precise through an example as shown in Figure 2.1, let node n_i be linked to nodes (n_j, n_k, n_l, n_m) (we drop the superscript since the camera identity is not needed). At time t, n_i has feature vectors $\mathcal{F}_{i,t} = \{\mathbf{F}_{n,t_j} | n = (j, k, l, m), t - t_W < t_j \le t\}$, where t_W is the width of the time window. Note that these observations from neighboring nodes are available only at discrete instants of time, i.e., t_j is a discrete variable. In practice, whenever a person exits a camera view that information is sent by the camera to all the other cameras linked to it based on the network architecture. Thus, (n_j, n_k, n_l, n_m) are all exit nodes and n_i is an entry node.

When a node n_i encounters a new observation at time t, it transforms it into a feature vector $\mathbf{F}_{n,t}$. Then, it estimates the similarity of this feature vector with its stored feature vectors, $\mathcal{F}_{i,t}$, obtained from neighboring nodes. For example, the similarity can be estimated using (2.6). Thus, the tracking task can be formulated as an association problem which maximizes similarities of the associated observations.

2.3   A REVIEW ON CAMERA NETWORK TRACKING

Some of the earlier methods on tracking in a camera network include [Huang and Russel, 1997, Javed et al., 2003, Kettnaker and Zabih, 1999]. In [Huang and Russel, 1997], a probabilistic approach was presented for finding corresponding vehicles across cameras on a highway. The appearance of vehicles was modeled by the mean of the color and transition times were modeled as Gaussian distributions. A Bayesian formulation of the problem of reconstructing the path of objects across multiple non-overlapping cameras was presented in [Kettnaker and Zabih, 1999] using color histograms for object appearance. A graph-theoretic framework for addressing the problem of tracking in a network of cameras was presented in [Javed et al., 2003]. The correspondences of tracks between different camera views were constructed using a bipartite graph matching strategy. The authors in [Rahimi and Darrell, 2004] used location and velocity of objects moving across multiple non-overlapping cameras to estimate the calibration parameters of the cameras and target trajectories. In [Leoputra et al., 2006], a particle filter was used to switch between track prediction for non-overlapping cameras and tracking within a camera. In [Kang et al., 2004], the authors presented a method for tracking in overlapping stationary and pan-tilt-zoom (PTZ) cameras by maximizing a joint motion and appearance probability model. An on-line learned discriminative appearance affinity model using Multiple Instance Learning was proposed in [Kuo et al., 2010] for associating multi-target tracks across multiple non-overlapping cameras.

Tracking in camera networks is closely related to person re-identification in camera networks. In [Gray and Tao, 2008], a machine learning algorithm was used to find the best feature representation of objects, where many different kinds of simple features can be combined into a single similarity function. In [Prosser et al., 2010], person reidentification across disjoint camera views was reformulated as a ranking problem. By learning a subspace where the potential true match is given the highest ranking, the problem was solved using a Ensemble RankSVM. The work by [Doretto et al., 2011] in this area is described in some detail below. A Cross Canonical Correlation Analysis framework was formulated in [Loy et al., 2009] to detect and quantify temporal and causal relationships between regional activities within and across camera views. In [Farenzena et al., 2010], the authors presented an appearance-based method for person reidentification. It consists of extraction and fusion of features that model three complementary aspects of the human appearance: the overall chromatic content, the spatial arrangement of colors into stable regions, and the presence of recurrent local motifs with high entropy. A spatiotemporal segmentation algorithm was employed in [Gheissari et al., 2006] to generate salient edgels (pixels in an image that have the characteristics of an edge) and invariant signatures were generated by combining normalized color and salient edgel histograms for establishing correspondence across camera views. In [Song and Roy-Chowdhury, 2008], a multi-objective optimization framework was presented for tracking in a camera network. It was shown that a stochastic graph evolution strategy could lead to robust tracking in a camera network. Adapting the feature correspondence computations by modeling the long-term dependencies between them and then obtaining the statistically optimal paths for each person was the proposed approach. There has also been recent work on tracking people in a multi-camera setup [Du and Piater, 2007, Khan and Shah, 2006] by exploiting the principal axes of the targets or using a planar homography constraint.

Next, we briefly review a few recent approaches that look at various aspects of the problem of tracking in a camera network. The paper [Kuo et al., 2010] proposes a Multiple Instance Learning (MIL) approach for an appearance-based affinity model between features in different cameras. The paper [Song et al., 2010a] trades-off on-line performance with accuracy in a setting where prior training data is not available and proposes a stochastic graph evolution framework for associating between tracklets. Person reidentification is an essential characteristic of any multi-camera wide-area tracking method with non-overlapping fields of view; the paper [Doretto et al., 2011] proposes a solution for this. Learning the traffic patterns between the views of non-overlapping cameras can produce essential information for the tracker and improve its performance over time. Some approaches that deal with issue are described in Section 2.7. The topology of a wide-area camera network would, in general, include both overlapping and non-overlapping fields of view. The work in [Khan and Shah, 2003] addresses the issue of associating targets seen in multiple views simultaneously.

2.4   ON-LINE LEARNING USING AFFINITY MODELS

Tracking over a camera network can be formulated as finding the correspondences between the tracklets obtained in different single cameras. Given the video observations, the goal is to associate tracklets so as to maximize a joint association probability. Therefore, one of the key components is the affinity between tracklets. To model affinities, usually two main cues are considered: the spatio-temporal information and appearance relationships. For non-overlapping camera networks, appearance cues may be more reliable compared to spatio-temporal information. An online learning approach was proposed in [Kuo et al., 2010] for modeling discriminative appearance affinities across cameras.

As the hand-labeled correspondences are not available at runtime, collecting training examples is difficult. In [Kuo et al., 2010], the spatio-temporal constraints are considered to collect online training samples, which are termed as "weakly labeled samples". A training sample is defined as a pair of tracklets from two cameras. Negative samples are the pairs of tracklets which overlap in time. Pairs of tracklets which have the potential to link constitute a positive "bag". Then Multiple Instance Learning (MIL) is applied to learn an appearance affinity model.

APPEARANCE AFFINITY MODELS WITH MULTIPLE INSTANCE LEARNING

Multiple Instance Learning is a variation on supervised learning. Instead of receiving a set of instances which are labeled positive or negative, the learner receives a set of bags that are labeled positive or negative. Each bag contains many instances. A bag is labeled negative if all the instances in it are negative. On the other hand, a bag is labeled positive if there is at least one instance in it which is positive. A MIL boosting algorithm selects weak classifiers and their corresponding weighted coefficients and then combines them into a strong classifier.

Training sample collection

If a pair of tracklets T_j^a in camera C^a and T_k^b in camera C^b are impossible to link according to spatio-temporal constraints, the pair is put into a negative "bag" and labeled "-1"; otherwise, the pair of tracklets can be possibly linked and is put into a positive"bag" and labeled "+1". Thus, the positive and negative training sample set can be denoted as

$$\mathcal{B}^+ = \left\{ x_i : \{T_j^a, T_k^b\}, y_i : +1 \right\}$$
$$\mathcal{B}^- = \left\{ x_i : \{T_j^a, T_k^b\}, y_i : -1 \right\},$$

where x_i represents a training sample and y_i is its label.

Appearance model representation

Three complementary features are considered. Color histograms are used to represent the color appearance in an image patch. Covariance matrices of image features are used to describe the image texture. The Histogram of Gradients (HOG) feature is chosen to capture shape information.

Multiple Instance Learning

In MIL, training samples are not labeled individually, but the label is given to each bag. Let x_{ij} denote an individual sample, where i is the index for the bag and j is the index for the sample within the bag. The label of each bag is denoted by y_i, where $y_i \in \{0, 1\}$. The goal is to learn the instance classifier which takes the form

$$H(x_{ij}) = \sum_{t=1}^{T} \alpha_t h_t(x_{ij}), \tag{2.7}$$

where $h(x)$ is a weak classifier. $h(x)$ is normalized to be in the restricted range $[-1, +1]$. The sign of $h(x)$ is the predicted label and the magnitude represents the confidence in this prediction. The probability of a sample x_{ij} being positive is defined as

$$p_{ij} = \frac{1}{1 + \exp(-y_{ij})}, \tag{2.8}$$

where $y_{ij} = H(x_{ij})$. The probability of a bag being positive is defined as

$$p_i = 1 - \prod_j (1 - p_{ij}). \tag{2.9}$$

An MIL boosting algorithm trains a boosting classifier that maximizes the log likelihood of bags, i.e.,

$$\log L(H) = \sum_i y_i \log p_i + (1 - y_i) \log(1 - p_i). \tag{2.10}$$

Then the weight of each sample is given as the derivative of the loss function $\log L(H)$ with respect to the score of that sample y_{ij}, i.e.,

$$w_{ij} = \frac{\partial \log L(H)}{\partial y_{ij}} = \frac{y_i - p_i}{p_i} p_{ij}. \tag{2.11}$$

The optimal weak classifier h_t and weighted coefficient α_t in the t-th boosting round, i.e.,

$$(\alpha_t, h_t) = \arg \min_{h, \alpha} \log L(H_{t-1} + \alpha h) \tag{2.12}$$

can be estimated through a gradient descent process.

The prediction confidence output by this classifier is combined with other cues (e.g., spatial correspondence and time interval) to compute the affinity between tracks for association.

Tracking Results

Some tracking results using this method are shown in Figure 2.2 [Kuo et al., 2010]. The videos used are captured in a campus environment.

2.5   TRACKLET ASSOCIATION USING STOCHASTIC SEARCH

In this section, we describe a stochastic search framework for computing the associations between tracklets in individual cameras. We refer readers to [Song et al., 2010a] and [Song and Roy-Chowdhury, 2008] for more details. The method can deal with hand-off between cameras and appearance variations over time.

Figure 2.3 shows an overview of the scheme. The method begins by identifying tracklets, i.e., the short-term fragments with low probability of error. In multi-camera network, the tracklets

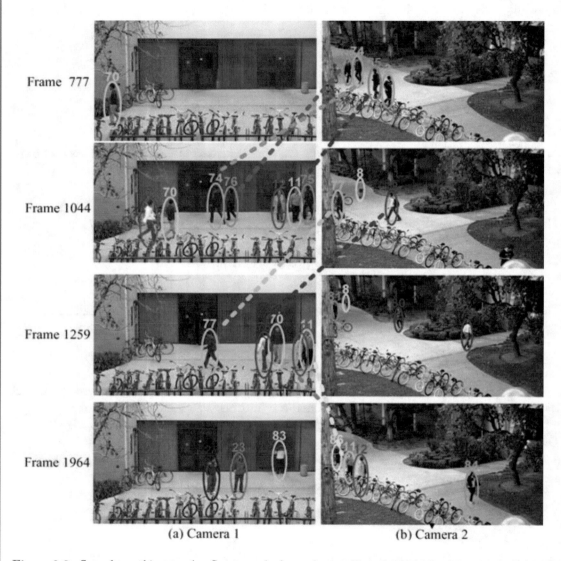

Figure 2.2: Sample tracking results. Some tracked people travelling through the cameras are linked by dotted lines. For example, the targets with IDs of 74, 75, and 76 leave Camera 2 around the same time. This method finds the correct association when they enter Camera 1. (From [Kuo et al., 2010])

are the intra-camera tracking results obtained using any single view tracker, for example, particle filter [Isard and Blake, 1998] or mean-shift tracker [Comaniciu et al., 2003]. The tracklets are then associated based on their affinities.

Using the affinity model, a tracklet association graph (TAG) is created with the tracklets as nodes and affinity scores as weights. The association of the tracklets can be found by computing the optimal paths in the graph. By splitting the beginning and end of each tracklet into two subsets, the problem of the tracklet association can be formulated as a maximum matching problem in a weighted bipartite graph [Javed et al., 2003]. The Hungarian algorithm [Kuhn, 1955] can be used to find the maximum matching.

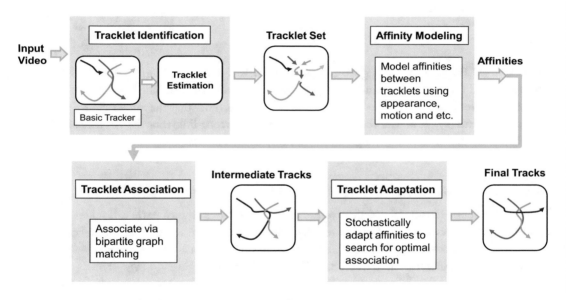

Figure 2.3: Overview of stochastic graph evolution framework. (From [Song et al., 2010a])

The tracking problem can be solved optimally by the above tracklet association method if the affinity scores were known exactly and assumed to be independent. However, this can be a big assumption due to well known low-level image processing challenges, like poor lighting conditions or unexpected motion of the targets. It is not uncommon for some of the similarities to be estimated wrongly since they depend on detected features which is not a perfect process. As shown in Figure 2.4, if the similarity estimation is incorrect for one pair of tracklets, the overall inferred long track may be wrong even if all the other tracklets are connected correctly. This leads to a development of a graph evolution scheme, in which the weights (i.e., affinity scores) on the edges of the tracklet association graph are adapted by measuring the similarity of observed features along a path that is generated after tracklet association. The authors in Song et al. [2010a] adopt the affinity adaptation method proposed in [Song and Roy-Chowdhury, 2008], but instead of adapting deterministically which may be stuck at a local optimum, they propose a Metropolis-Hastings based adaptation scheme with the potential to reach the global optimum.

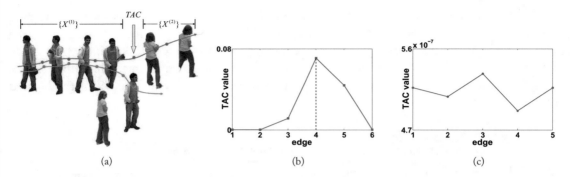

| (a) | (b) | (c) |

Figure 2.4: (a) Tracklets of two targets: ground truth track of the person in green T-shirt is shown with orange line, and the association results before adaptation are shown with blue line. (b)-(c): TAC values along the incorrect and correct association results, respectively, (note that the range of the y-axis in (c) is much smaller than (b)). It is clear that TAC has a peak at the wrong link; thus the variance of TAC along the wrongly associated tracklets is higher than the correct one. (From [Song et al., 2010a])

TRACKLET ASSOCIATION THROUGH STOCHASTIC GRAPH EVOLUTION

To model the spatio-temporal variation of the observed features along a path, a Tracklet Association Cost (TAC) is defined. Given an estimated track for the qth target, λ_q, TAC is defined on each edge $e_{ij} \in \lambda_q$. The feature vector of the tracklets before (in time) e_{ij} on λ_q and those after e_{ij} are treated as two clusters. An illustration of TAC calculation is shown in Figure 2.4 (a).

Let $\{X\}$ be the set of feature (e.g., appearance) of all N tracklets along the path and let them be clustered into $\{X^{(1)}\}$ and $\{X^{(2)}\}$ with respect to each edge $e_{ij} \in \lambda_q$. Let the mean m of the features in $\{X\}$ be $m = \frac{1}{N} \sum_{x \in \{X\}} x$. Let m_i be the mean of N_i data points of class $\{X^{(i)}\}$, $i = 1, 2$, such that $m_i = \frac{1}{N_i} \sum_{x \in \{X^{(i)}\}} x$. Let S_T be the variance of the all observed feature x along the path, i.e., $S_T = \sum_{x \in \{X\}} |x - m|^2$ and S_W be the sum of the variances along each sub-path, $\{X^{(1)}\}$ and $\{X^{(2)}\}$, i.e., $S_W = \sum_{i=1}^{2} S_i = \sum_{i=1}^{2} \sum_{x \in \{X^{(i)}\}} |x - m_i|^2$. The TAC for e_{ij} is defined as

$$TAC(e_{ij}) = \frac{|S_T - S_W|}{|S_W|} \triangleq \frac{|S_B|}{|S_W|}. \tag{2.13}$$

Thus, the TAC is defined from Fisher's linear discriminant function [Duda et al., 2001] and measures the ratio of the distance between different clusters, S_B, over the distances between the members within each cluster S_W. If all the feature nodes along a path belong to the same target, the value of TAC at each edge $e_{ij} \in \lambda_q$ should be low, and thus the variance of TAC over all the edges along the path should also be low. If the feature nodes belonging to different people are connected wrongly, we will get a higher value of TAC at the wrong link, and the variance of TAC along the path will be higher. Thus, the distribution of TAC along a path can be used to detect if there is a wrong connection along that path.

The authors then design a loss function for determining the final tracks by analyzing features along a path. They specify the function in terms of the TAC function and adapt the affinity scores to minimize

$$L(\lambda_q) = \sum_{\lambda_q} Var(TAC(e_{ij} \in \lambda_q)). \tag{2.14}$$

Metropolis-Hastings based Adaptation of Tracklet Association

Whenever there is a peak in the TAC function for some edge along a path, the validity of the connections between the features along that path is under doubt. As per the Metropolis-Hastings method, this leads to a new candidate affinity score s'_{ij} on this edge where the peak occurs using a proposal distribution $q_{af}(s'_{ij}|s_{ij})$, where s_{ij} is the affinity score on edge e_{ij}. The proposal distribution $q_{af}(s'_{ij}|s_{ij})$ is chosen to be an uniform distribution of width 2δ, i.e., $U(s_{ij} - \delta, s_{ij} + \delta)$, since without additional information, uniform distribution can be a reasonable guess of the new weights. Any other distribution can be chosen based on the application.

It is then possible to recalculate the maximum matching paths, λ'_q, of the new feature graph. The target probability $p_{af}(.)$ is defined as

$$p_{af}(s_{ij}) \propto \exp(-L(\lambda_q)), \quad p_{af}(s'_{ij}) \propto \exp(-L(\lambda'_q)) . \tag{2.15}$$

The candidate weight s'_{ij} is accepted with probability $\rho_{af}(s_{ij}, s'_{ij})$ as

$$\rho_{af}(s_{ij}, s'_{ij}) = \min \left\{ \frac{p_{af}(s'_{ij})q_{af}(s_{ij}|s'_{ij})}{p_{af}(s_{ij})q_{af}(s'_{ij}|s_{ij})}, 1 \right\} . \tag{2.16}$$

In practice, if $s'_{ij} \geq s_{ij}$, the maximum matching result will not change, i.e., $\lambda'_q = \lambda_q$, so the candidate weight s'_{ij} is accepted with probability 1. However, in this case, the adaptation scheme will not achieve any gain from the new proposal since it has the same maximum matching result. Thus, we can discard the proposed s'_{ij} if $s'_{ij} \geq s_{ij}$, and keep proposing until $s'_{ij} < s_{ij}$, and then recalculate the maximum matching paths.

The adaptation scheme is summarized below.

1. Construct a weighted graph G, where the vertices are the tracklets and edge weights are the affinities.

2. Estimate the optimal paths, λ_q based on bipartite graph matching.

3. Compute the TAC for each $e_{ij} \in \lambda_q$.

4. Propose a weight s'_{ij} on the link where the TAC peak occurs based on a proposal distribution.

5. Recalculate the maximum matching paths, λ'_q, of the new feature graph. We accept the new graph with probability $\rho_{af}(s_{ij}, s'_{ij})$ in (2.16).

6. Repeat Steps 4 and 5 until either a predefined iteration number is reached or the system reaches some predefined stopping criterion.

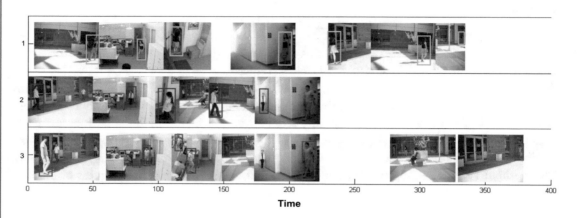

Figure 2.5: Example of some of the images of the people in the network. The horizontal axis is the time when these images were observed, while the vertical axis is the index of the persons. The tracks of 3 of the targets are shown in different colors and clearly demonstrate the ability to deal with hand off in non-overlapping cameras. (From [Song et al., 2011c])

We now show some results on tracking in a camera network using the stochastic graph evolution framework as described in detail in [Song and Roy-Chowdhury, 2008]. The network consists of 7 cameras and 26 entry/exist nodes. The cameras are installed in both indoor and outdoor environments which consist of large illumination and appearance changes. We considered 9 people moving across the network for about 7 min. Examples of some of the images of 3 persons with tracking results are shown in Figure 2.5. Note the significant changes of appearance. The results thus demonstrate the ability to track with handoffs. Tracking in large camera networks is still in the process of maturing and there do not exist standard datasets to compare performance of various methods. The recently released camera network dataset [Denina et al., 2011] can provide such an evaluation benchmark in the future.

2.6   PERSON REIDENTIFICATION

The problem of person reidentification in a camera network is to link people detected in different views or at different time instants to the same individuals. It is a fundamental problem for video analysis in a large-scale network of cameras. The work in [Doretto et al., 2011] focuses on reidentifying a person based on the whole body appearance of an individual. By assuming that a person will not change his clothes during a blind gap between cameras, the cue of overall body appearance can be exploited for identity management. To fulfill this aim, a signature representing the person, which should be distinctive and invariant to changes in illumination, viewpoint, pose and clothing appearance, needs to be computed from the appearance information.

Computing local descriptors and then integrating them is a typical way of building appearance models. Different local descriptors and integration strategies lead to different appearance modeling approaches. Local descriptors can be aggregated either in a *holistic* way to represent the whole-body appearance or using *parts-based* methods that divide the body into regions and, therefore, a parts-matching mechanism is required. A histogram-based model is natural for holistically representing appearance. To account for the limitation of histogram-based models for capturing higher-order information, such as the spatial distribution of local descriptors, a *appearance context model* was proposed in [Doretto et al., 2011]. The appearance context model is a holistic representation that describes the co-occurrence of appearance labels to capture their spatial distribution. Part identification and correspondence can be carried out in different ways; for example, matching based on interest points, or fitting a model to identify body parts and establishing a mapping from one individual to another. In [Doretto et al., 2011], a *shape and appearance context* model was also proposed, which is a parts-based method that extends the appearance context by using body parts explicitly to improve distinctiveness.

LOCAL DESCRIPTOR

The local descriptor in [Doretto et al., 2011] was calculated by applying basic operations to the pixels. Let I be an image. The descriptor at the pixel x was denoted as $\varphi(x)$, which is a r-dimensional vector, i.e., $\varphi(x) = [\varphi_1(x), \ldots, \varphi_r(x)]^T$. Two descriptors were considered: the *histogram of oriented gradients in the Log-RGB color space* (or HOG Log-RGB, in short), and the *hue, saturation, and edgel* values (or HSV-edgel, in short).

HOG Log-RGB local descriptor.   The HOG Log-RGB can be represented mathematically as

$$\varphi(x) = \begin{bmatrix} \mathrm{HOG}(\nabla \log(I_R), x) \\ \mathrm{HOG}(\nabla \log(I_G), x) \\ \mathrm{HOG}(\nabla \log(I_B), x) \end{bmatrix}, \tag{2.17}$$

where I_R, I_G, I_B are the R, G, B channels of the image I and $\mathrm{HOG}(\cdot, x)$ computes the histogram of oriented gradients on a region of $w \times w$ pixels around x.

HSV-edgel local descriptor.   In this descriptor, the color information is captured by the hue and saturation values of a pixel and the structure information is represented by a description of the pixel that has the characteristics of an edge, and is referred to as an *edgel*. Therefore, the descriptor is represented mathematically as

$$\varphi(x) = [I_H(x), I_S(x), \angle e(x), e_R(x), e_G(x), e_B(x)]^T, \tag{2.18}$$

where I_H and I_S represent the hue and saturation, and e indicate the edgel. The angle $\angle e(x)$ is the dominant local boundary orientation. As the structural appearance of loose fitting or wrinkled clothing is highly dynamic, traditional edge operator will produce many spurious edges. To address this issue, a spatiotemporal segmentation algorithm is applied to the image to generate salient edgels corresponding to the boundaries of each type of clothing.

HISTOGRAM-BASED APPEARANCE MODEL

Bounding box model.   In this model, the HSV-edgel descriptor for every foreground pixel is computed and then a histogram is computed. The histogram is the concatenation of two parts. The first one performs the frequency count of the jointly quantized hue and saturation channels, I_H and I_S. The second part represents the structural qualities of the region through the edgels. For matching, the distance between two models is defined by the intersection histogram [Swain and Ballard, 1991].

Bag-of-features model.   In this model, the HOG Log-RGB descriptor at every foreground pixel is computed and a vector quantization is performed on the descriptor. Then a histogram of the quantization labels is computed. For matching, two models are compared with the L_1 norm.

APPEARANCE CONTEXT MODELING

A major limitation of all the holistic models based on histograms is that they lose the spatial distribution information of the appearance labels. To address this issue, an appearance context model was proposed in [Doretto et al., 2011], which not only computes the histogram of appearance but also describes how they are distributed by evaluating their spatial co-occurrence.

Let $S : \Lambda \to \mathcal{S}$ and $A : \Lambda \to \mathcal{A}$ be two functions defined on a discrete domain Λ of dimensions $M \times N$ and assuming values in the label sets $\mathcal{S} = \{s_1, \ldots, s_n\}$ and $\mathcal{A} = \{a_1, \ldots, a_m\}$. Let $\mathcal{P} = \{p_1, \ldots, p_l\}$ be a partition such that $\bigcup_i p_i$ represents a plane and $p_i \cap p_j = \emptyset$ for $i \neq j$. Given $p \in \mathcal{P}$ and a point on plane $\mathbf{x}$, $p(\mathbf{x})$ indicates the partition element p translated by $\mathbf{x}$, i.e., $p(\mathbf{x}) = \{\mathbf{x} + \mathbf{y} | \mathbf{y} \in p\}$). $h(a, p(x))$ indicates the histogram of the labels of A located in the region $p(\mathbf{x})$, i.e., $h(a, p(\mathbf{x})) = P(A(\mathbf{z}) = a | \mathbf{z} \in p(\mathbf{x}))$. Let D_s indicate the set of points $\mathbf{x}$ with label $s \in S$, i.e., $D_s = \{\mathbf{x} | S(\mathbf{x}) = s\}$. Then, we can define the *occurrence* function as follows. The *occurrence* function $\Theta : \mathcal{A} \times \mathcal{S} \times \mathcal{P} \to \mathbb{R}_+$ is such that the point (a, s, p) maps to

$$\Theta(a, s, p) = E[h(a, p(\mathbf{x})) | D_s], \tag{2.19}$$

where $E[\cdot | D]$ indicates expectation with respect to a random variable $\mathbf{x}$ which has an uniform distribution in D. The meaning of the occurrence function is the following: Given S and A for a label $s = S(\mathbf{x})$, the histogram of the labels $\mathcal{A}$ over the region $p(\mathbf{x})$ on average is given by $\Theta(\cdot, s, p)$. When $\mathcal{S} = \mathcal{A}$ and $S(\mathbf{x}) = A(\mathbf{x})$, Θ is referred to as *co-occurrence*. It means that, for a label $a = A(\mathbf{x})$, the histogram of labels over the region $p(\mathbf{x})$ on average is $\Theta(\cdot, a, p)$.

This model is obtained by first computing the local descriptor and performing quantization steps, same as the bag-of-feature model. The model captures the spatial arrangement of the appearance in the sense that for a label a, the co-occurrence $\Theta(\cdot, a, p)$ encodes the probability distribution of the labels in several spatial regions p, relative to the label a. In order to perform fast occurrence computation, a procedure that leverages on a generalization of the integral representation of images is developed (see [Doretto et al., 2011] for more details).

PARTS-BASED MODELING BY INTEREST POINT MATCHING

In this parts-based appearance model, an interest operator is used to identify parts and establish correspondences between individuals. Given an image of a person, the Hessian affine invariant interest operator [Mikolajczyk and Schmid, 2005] is used to nominate points of interest. When two images I and J are compared, an initial set of correspondences are nominated. The merit of a potential match $(i \rightarrow j)$ is evaluated using the intersection histogram. Inverse matching is used to ensure consistency of the correspondences.

PARTS-BASED MODELING BY MODEL FITTING

A model-based approach that generates a correspondence between different body parts such as the head, arms, legs and torso is considered. A decomposable triangulated graph is used for modeling and segmenting people in a scene using an energy minimization approach.

Once the model fitting is done, the appearance model for an individual is computed as follows. The individual is partitioned into salient body parts using the fitted model. Using all the triangles that correspond to the upper torso, the appearance and structure is described by a histogram of the same type that is used in the bounding box model, which is based on the spatiotemporal HSV-edgel local descriptor. Similarly, the signatures for all the other body parts are computed and compared using histogram intersection.

SHAPE AND APPEARANCE CONTEXT MODELING

This is an extension of the appearance context model. It is computed with respect to specific parts of the body of an individual and makes the appearance model more distinctive.

Given the image I, let A be its appearance labeled image, and let S (defined over Λ) be its shape labeled image. Then the shape and appearance context model of I is the occurrence Θ computed over S and A, which is an $m \times n \times l$ matrix. Here, m and n are the number of appearance labels and shape labels respectively, and l is the number of partitions. The matching of two shape and appearance context models is done via the L_1 norm.

2.7   LEARNING A CAMERA NETWORK TOPOLOGY

To successfully track an object in a camera network, the environment in which the cameras operate usually needs to be learned. However, prior information, such as color, spatial or environmental calibration, may not be available beforehand. Ideally, a tracking system should be able to: (i) work immediately upon initialization; (ii) improve its performance as new evidence becomes available; and, (iii) adapt to changes in the operating environment. In a camera network with non-overlapping fields of view, knowledge about the possible trajectories that targets can follow in the "blind" areas, can significantly improve the tracking performance. This has been referred to as the problem of learning a camera network topology (here topology refers to the traffic flow patterns, rather than the communication paths). Inference of the topology requires tracking; in turn, as more knowledge about the traffic patterns is gleaned from the data, the tracking performance should improve over time.

Several authors have studied this problem, e.g., [Gilbert and Bowden, 2008, Markis et al., 2004, Tieu et al., 2005, Zou et al., 2009]. Similar problem has also been addressed by learning the activity correlation [Loy et al., 2010] (see Section 4.2 for details). Below we describe the basic ideas behind the solution strategies that have been proposed. To fix the description to a particular feature vector, we adopt the notation of [Gilbert and Bowden, 2008].

COLOR-BASED INTER-CAMERA COUPLING

In each camera, the static background modeling is used to detect moving objects, and then the Kalman filter is used to track each of them. Once the foreground objects have been segmented, a color descriptor is formed to provide the appearance model of that object. The Consensus-Color Conversion of Munsell (CCCM) is selected as the color space [Sturges and Whitfield, 1995]. CCCM works by breaking the RGB color space into 11 discrete colors. Each basic color represents a perceptual color category established through a physiological study of how human's categorize color. The appearance of an object is modeled by the median CCCM color histogram over its entire trajectory within a single camera, and is denoted as $B = (b_1, b_2, ..., b_n)$. The key assumption here is that, given time, objects (such as people or cars) will follow similar routes between cameras due to geographical paths, shortest routes and obstructions. All new objects that are detected are compared to previous objects exiting other cameras within a set time window, T.

Given objects i and j, their color correlation is computed using histogram intersection as

$$H_{ij} = \sum_{k=1}^{11} \min(B_{ik}, B_{jk}). \tag{2.20}$$

Thus, the frequency, f, of a bin, ϕ, of a histogram representing reappearance periods is calculated as

$$f_\phi = \sum_{\forall i} \sum_{\forall j} \begin{cases} H_{ij} G(t_j^{start} - t_i^{end} - \phi\mu), & \phi\mu \le (t_j^{start} - t_i^{end}) < (\phi + 1)\mu \\ 0 & \text{otherwise} \end{cases} \quad \forall \phi, \phi\mu < T, \tag{2.21}$$

where t_i^{start} and t_i^{end} are the entry and exit times of object i, respectively, T is the maximum allowable reappearance period, and μ is the bin size in seconds. G is a 1D Gaussian kernel which is introduced to reduce the effect of different quantization levels.

Frequencies are only calculated for objects that disappear from region y followed by reappearances in region x, and are denoted as $f^{x|y}$. Then, an approximation of the conditional transition probability $P(O_{x,t}|O_y)$ is obtained by

$$P(O_{x,t}|O_y) = \frac{f_t^{x|y}}{\sum_{\phi=0}^{\lfloor T/\mu \rfloor} f_\phi^{x|y}}, \tag{2.22}$$

where $O_{x,t}$ is the object observed in region x at time t.

After sufficient evidence has been accumulated, the noise floor level is measured for each link. If the maximum peak of the distribution is found to exceed the noise floor level, this indicates a possible coupling between the regions. In order to allow for multiple entry and exit areas, the field-of-view of each camera is split into a number of equal regions (16 as set in [Gilbert and Bowden, 2008]). As the links between regions are incrementally learned, the posterior for a newly detected object i in region x being object j in region y can be given by

$$P(O_y^j|O_x^i) = H_{ij} P(O_{x,t_i^{start}-t_j^{end}}|O_y). \tag{2.23}$$

Tracking of objects is then achieved by maximizing the posterior probability within a time window.

The CCCM color quantization descriptor assumes a similar color response between cameras. However, this is seldom the case in practice. Therefore, a transformation matrix is formed incrementally to model the color changes between cameras by automatically utilizing the tracked people as the calibration objects. This transformation is computed via SVD in the RGB space (see [Gilbert and Bowden, 2008] for more details).

SIZE-BASED INTER-CAMERA COUPLING

As it is assumed that, over time, objects follow similar routes between cameras, they will leave and enter cameras in consistent areas and therefore the size of the object should be consistent upon entry and exit. This observation can be utilized to calculate the likelihood that a person has come from another camera based upon the relative entry size to the current camera. Similar to the previous section, the frequency of a histogram representing two observations in two cameras being linked based on the size of their bounding boxes can be calculated as

$$f(size_i^{exit}, size_j^{entry}) = \sum_{\forall i} \sum_{\forall j} H_{ij} G(size_i^{exit}, size_j^{entry}) \quad \text{if } (t_j^{start} - t_i^{end}) < T, \tag{2.24}$$

where G is a 2D Gaussian kernel. Then, the conditional probability of the resulting change in bounding box size $P(O_{x,Entry}|O_{y,Exit})$ is estimated by normalizing f. This is then used to weight the observation likelihood obtained through color similarity as was done in the previous section.

2.8   CONSISTENT LABELING WITH OVERLAPPING FIELDS OF VIEW

The consistent labeling problem is to establish correspondence between tracks of the same object, seen in different cameras, to recover complete information about the object. In a network of cameras with overlapping fields of view, if the cameras are calibrated and the environment model is known, consistent labeling can be established by projecting the location of each 3D object to the world coordinate system, and establishing equivalence between objects that project to the same location. However, in most situations, the calibrated cameras or environment models are not available. A framework that solves the consistent labeling problem using uncalibrated cameras was described in [Khan and Shah, 2003]. This approach is built on finding the limits of the field-of-view (FOV) of each camera as visible in the other cameras, which are called field-of-view lines. It was shown in [Khan and Shah, 2003] that, if the FOV lines are known, it is possible to disambiguate between multiple possibilities for correspondence. In this section, we briefly review this framework.

FIELD OF VIEW LINES

It is assumed that (i) the ground plane is visible in all cameras; (ii) all the sequences are time-aligned; and (iii) the cameras have overlapping FOVs. The image seen in the ith camera is denoted as $C^i(x, y)$. The FOV of C^i is a rectangular pyramid in space with its tip at the optical center of the camera, and with its four sides passing through the lines ($x = 0, x = x_{\max}, y = 0, y = y_{\max}$) on the image plane. The intersection of each planar side of this rectangular pyramid with the ground plane marks the boundaries of the footprint of the image. This is called a 3D FOV line. A projection of this 3D FOV line marking the limit of the footprint may be visible in another camera. The sides of a camera image can be defined by four lines, and s is used to denote an arbitrary side of these four. If $L^{i,s}$ is a 3D FOV line, which marks the viewing limit of C^i from side s, then $L^{i,s}_j$ is the 2D FOV line of side s of C^i in C_j.

Computing the Visibility of an Object in Another Camera. The kth object seen in C^i is denoted as O^i_k, and its location is approximated by the bottom center of its bounding box, i.e., $(x^i_k, y^i_k) = \mathfrak{p}(O^i_k)$, where $\mathfrak{p}(O^i_k)$ returns the single point representing the location of the center of the bottom of the bounding box of the object.

The consistent labeling task is to establish equivalences in the form $O^i_m \leftrightarrow O^j_n$. If the FOV lines are known, each line, $L^{i,s}_j$, divides the image into two parts - one is inside the FOV of C^i and the other is outside. The function $L^{i,s}_j(x, y)$ returns greater than 0 if the point (x, y) lies on the side of $L^{i,s}_j$ that should be visible in C^i, less than 0 if it is not visible in C^i, and equal to 0 if it is on the line. The set of cameras $\mathbf{C}$ in which O^i_k will be visible is

$$\mathbf{C}_i(k) = \{j | L^{j,s}_i(\mathfrak{p}(O^i_k)) > 0\}. \tag{2.25}$$

Establishing Consistent Labeling. Once the set of cameras $\mathbf{C}$ in which the current object should be visible is known, the match among the objects seen in those cameras can be estimated. The process consists of applying the following FOV constraint to all the objects.

FOV Constraint. If a new view of an object is seen in C^i such that it has entered the image along side s, then the corresponding view of the same object will be visible on the line $L^{i,s}_j$ in C^j, provided

$j \in \mathbf{C}_i$. Moreover, the direction of motion of this corresponding view will be such that the function $L_j^{i,s}(x', y')$ changes from negative to positive.

Based on this constraint, a short list of the candidates for possible correspondence can be generated. The objects viewed in different cameras are then associated by

$$O_m^i \leftrightarrow O_n^{j'} \quad \text{if } n, j' = \arg\min_{p,j} D(L_j^{i,s}, O_p^j) \quad \forall j \in \mathbf{C}_i(m), \tag{2.26}$$

where p is the label of objects in C^j and $D(L, O)$ is the distance of object O from a line L.

Once equivalences of $O_m^i \leftrightarrow O_n^j$ between views of the same object have been established, we have essentially established a correspondence between the entire tracks in the two views. Then the homography between these two views can be estimated.

AUTOMATIC DETERMINATION OF FOV LINES

When there are multiple people in the scene and someone enters/exits the FOV of a camera, all persons in other cameras are picked as being candidates for the projection of the FOV line. False candidates are randomly spread on both sides of the line, whereas the correct candidates are clustered on a single line. Therefore, the Hough transform can be applied to find the best line. However, it is not an uncommon situation where one of the edges of the current camera's FOV is not visible in some other camera. In this case, all the correspondences marked will be incorrect. This may result in a wrong estimate of the line via the Hough Transform. To reduce the number of false correspondences, an *Invisibility Map* is generated. The binary invisibility map in C^i with respect to C^j is defined as the region of the image in C^i which is not visible in C^j. As an example, consider a camera pair C^i and C^j such that only one person is visible in C^i and nothing is visible in C^j. Then the location of the person in C^i is included in the invisibility map of C^i with respect to C^j. The process of generating Invisibility Map progressively reduces the number of false correspondences that are encountered, and its influence increases as more and more cases of sparse traffic within the environment are observed.

2.9   CONCLUSIONS

This chapter has described the problem of tracking in a camera network and a few strategies that address some of the important issues—robust feature extraction, error estimation and correction, object correspondences between cameras and continuous improvement of tracking performance over time. There are many other excellent approaches that have also been proposed for these problems. These are also the major directions of future research in this area. All the existing methods have significant assumptions and consistently high performance across various application domains is still elusive. Tracking from aerial videos where there is motion of the imaging platform and the object resolution is very low is another interesting scenario for researchers. Finally, standard databases for analyzing wide-area tracking results are not very common and need to be developed.

CHAPTER 3

Distributed Processing in Camera Networks

In many applications, it is desirable that the video analysis tasks be distributed over the network. There may not be enough bandwidth and transmission power available to send all the data to a central station. Furthermore, a single central station can bring down the entire network if it malfunctions and is prone to security threats. Also, centralized systems require setting up extensive communication and computation infrastructure prior to the actual operation of the network. This may be challenging in many field operations, like disaster management or operations in hostile environments. Distributed vision systems, possibly working alongside humans, can enlarge the application domain by facilitating operations in environments that may be too dangerous and hostile for humans.

In such situations, the cameras would have to act as autonomous agents making decisions in a decentralized manner. However, the individual decisions of the cameras need to be coordinated so that there is a consensus about the task (e.g., tracking, camera parameter assignment, activity recognition) even if each camera is an autonomous agent. Thus, the cameras need to analyze the raw data locally, exchange only distilled information that is relevant to the collaboration, and reach a shared, global analysis of the scene. Research in the area of distributed camera networks is very much in its early years and is a promising future direction, especially in the application domain of multi-agent systems equipped with video sensors.

We start by reviewing one of the most popular distributed estimation methods - the consensus approach. We then show how it can be applied to the problems of distributed tracking and distributed calibration and pose estimation. We envision a system where each of the cameras will have its own embedded processing unit capable of tasks like target detection, association and tracking. Through calibration, the geometrical relationships among the cameras can be constructed. The cameras need to have communication capabilities so that they can share information with each other.

3.1 CONSENSUS ALGORITHMS FOR DISTRIBUTED ESTIMATION

In the multi-agent systems literature, *consensus* means that the agents reach an agreement regarding a certain quantity of interest that depends on the measurements of all sensors in a network. The network may not be fully connected, so there is no central unit that has access to all the data from the sensors. Consequently, a *consensus algorithm* is an interaction rule that specifies information exchange between a sensor and its neighbors that guarantees that all the nodes reach a consensus.

The interaction topology of a network of sensors is represented using a graph $G = (V, E)$ with the set of nodes $V = \{1, 2, ..., n\}$ and edges $E \subseteq V \times V$. Each sensor node $i = 1, ..., n$ maintains an estimate $\mathbf{x}_i \in \mathbb{R}^m$ of a quantity $\mathbf{x} \in \mathbb{R}^m$. Consensus is achieved when $\mathbf{x}_1 = \mathbf{x}_2 = ... = \mathbf{x}_n$, which is an n-dimensional subspace of $\mathbb{R}^{mn}$. For example, in a network of temperature sensors, each sensor's estimates of temperature could be different due to noise and local variation. The sensors then interchange information with their neighboring sensors, and use the information to refine their local estimates. Consensus is reached when all sensors agree on a single value. A thorough review of consensus in networked multi-agent systems can be found in [Olfati-Saber et al., 2007].

Distributed computing [Lynch, 1996] has been an active research field for the last few decades. A lot of work has been done on consensus algorithms which formed the baseline for distributed computing. Formally the study of consensus originated in management science and statistics in 1960s (see [DeGroot, 1974]). The work in [Tsitsiklis et al., 1986] on asynchronous asymptotic agreement problems in distributed decision making systems and parallel computing [Bertsekas and Tsitsiklis, 1989] were initial pieces of work in this area. A theoretical framework for defining and solving consensus problems for networked dynamic systems was introduced in [Olfati-Saber and Murray, 2004] building on the earlier work of [Fax, 2001]. Consensus algorithms for reaching an agreement without computing any objective function appeared in the work of [Jadbabaie et al., 2003]. Further theoretical extensions of this work were presented in [Ren and Beard, 2005] with a focus towards treatment of directed information flow in networks. The setup in [Olfati-Saber and Murray, 2004] was originally created with the vision of designing agent-based amorphous computers for collaborative information processing in networks. Later, [Olfati-Saber and Murray, 2004] was used in development of flocking algorithms with guaranteed convergence and the capability to deal with obstacles and adversarial agents [Olfati-Saber, 2006]. Recent works related to multi agent networked systems include local control strategies [Lin et al., 2004], collective behavior of flocks and swarms [Olfati-Saber, 2006], sensor fusion [Olfati-Saber, 2007], random networks [Hatano and Mesbahi, 2005], synchronization of coupled oscillators [Preciado and Verghese, 2005], algebraic connectivity of complex networks [Olfati-Saber, 2005], asynchronous distributed algorithms [Mehyar et al., 2005], formation control for multi robot systems [Egerstedt and Hu, 2001], and dynamic graphs [Mesbahi, 2005].

The goals of most consensus algorithms usually include the following:

1. Validity: The final answer that achieves consensus is a valid answer.

2. Agreement: All agents agree on the final answer.

3. Termination: The consensus process eventually ends with each agent contributing.

4. Integrity: Agents vote only once.

Many consensus algorithms contain a series of events (and related messages) during a decision-making round. Typical events include Proposal and Decision. Here, proposal typically means the communication of the state of each agent and decision is the process of an agent deciding on proposals received from its neighbors. In our application domain of camera networks, the agents are the cameras and the state vector we are trying to estimate can be the position and velocity of a set of targets or the ID of an activity. In the remainder of this chapter, we will provide examples of consensus algorithms proposed for different video analysis applications, specifically on tracking, pose estimation and activity recognition. The Kalman consensus algorithm for distributed tracking in video will be analyzed in detail.

3.2   DECENTRALIZED AND DISTRIBUTED TRACKING

Based on inter-sensor communication, the trackers in a camera network can be categorized into three groups: centralized, decentralized and distributed tracking [Taj and Cavaliaro, 2011]. Centralized tracking is performed in a central processor which receives data from each camera in the network. In decentralized tracking schemes, the cameras are grouped into clusters, and each cluster has a local fusion center or group leader which gathers information of its group members. In distributed tracking, each camera performs its own estimation and exchanges information only with its immediate neighbors. There is no fusion center.

3.2.1   DECENTRALIZED TRACKING

In a decentralized tracking strategy, the group leader, which is the fusion center, collects raw or filtered data from other cameras in its group; then the fusion centers communicate with each other to accomplish tracking over the network. Thus, traditional trackers can be extended for decentralized tracking in multi-camera environments by incorporating the fusion centers. Some notable tracking algorithms are graph matching, particle filters, and Kalman filters. We discuss next how these algorithms are extended to a decentralized scenario.

Graph Matching
In Section 2.5, we described a graph matching based framework for tracking in a camera network by associating tracklets obtained in each camera. This framework can be applied on the fusion centers, which link the tracklets within each group and generate super-tracklets. Next, through communication between fusion centers, this graph matching framework can be applied to associate these super-tracklets and end up with the final tracks over the network.

Particle Filter
The basic idea of using particle filter for tracking was introduced in Section 2.1.2. In a decentralized camera network, each camera in a cluster can run individual particle filters to compute local state estimates that are then merged at the fusion center [Rosencrantz et al., 2003]. However, transferring particles and their weights across the network may introduce heavy communication load. It can be more efficient, in term of communication expense, to run one particle filter at the fusion center instead of running a particle filter at each camera node. Cameras transmit their measurements to associated fusion centers. The particles on each fusion center are propagated and a histogram of the expected measurement values is constructed. The measurements are then exchanged between all fusion centers to generate the global estimate of the target state [Kim and Davis, 2006].

Kalman Filter

A partially distributed target tracking approach using a cluster-based Kalman filter was proposed in [Medeiros et al., 2008]. Here, a camera is selected as a cluster head which aggregates all the measurements of a target to estimate its position using a Kalman filter and sends that estimate to a central base station.

3.2.2 DISTRIBUTED TRACKING

Unlike decentralized tracking, there is no fusion center in distributed tracking. Each camera node exchanges its estimates with its neighbors until a desired accuracy is reached.

In [Medeiros et al., 2008], a partially distributed target tracking approach using a cluster-based Kalman filter was proposed. Here, a camera is selected as a cluster head which aggregates all the measurements of a target to estimate its position using a Kalman filter and sends that estimate to a central base station. Due to the presence of cluster heads and a central station, this is not a completely distributed approach. A related work that deals with tracking targets in a camera network with PTZ cameras is [Qureshi and Terzopoulos, 2007]. Here, the authors proposed a mixture between a distributed and a centralized scheme using both static and PTZ cameras in a virtual camera network environment.

A distributed Kalman-Consensus filter, and subsequent variants, was proposed in [Olfati-Saber, 2007, 2009, Olfati-Saber and Sandell, 2008]. This was a completely distributed solution for estimating the dynamic state of a moving target. However, there are some major considerations in applying the method to camera networks due to the nature of video sensors. Cameras are directional sensors, each having a limited view of the entire theater of action, with the data having high bandwidth and complexity. We will next show how the basic approaches on consensus for distributed estimation in the multi-agent systems literature can be applied for designing a consensus-based tracking algorithm in camera networks.

3.3 CONSENSUS ALGORITHMS FOR DISTRIBUTED TRACKING

3.3.1 MATHEMATICAL FRAMEWORK

Let $\mathcal{C}$ be the set of all cameras in the network. We can then define the subset of all cameras viewing target T_j as $\mathcal{C}_j^v \subset \mathcal{C}$ and the rest of the cameras as $\mathcal{C}_j^{v-} \subset \mathcal{C}$. Each camera C_i will also have its set of *neighboring cameras* $\mathcal{C}_i^n \subset \mathcal{C}$. Based on the communication constraints due to bandwidth limitations and network connections, we define the set $\mathcal{C}_i^n$ as all the cameras with which C_i is able to communicate directly. In other words, C_i can assume that no cameras other than its neighbors, $\mathcal{C}_i^n$, exist as no information flows directly from non-neighboring cameras to C_i. Note that the set of neighbors need not be geographical neighbors. We also define the set of *overlapping cameras* of C_i as $\mathcal{C}_i^o \subset \mathcal{C}$; since all the cameras can change their PTZ parameters and have therefore several possible fields of view, we define the set $\mathcal{C}_i^o$ as all the cameras with which C_i can *potentially* have an

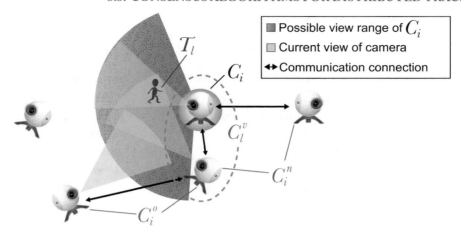

Figure 3.1: Conceptual illustration of camera network topologies. $\mathcal{C}_l^v \subset \mathcal{C}$ is the subset of all cameras viewing target T_l and the rest of the cameras are $\mathcal{C}_l^{v-} \subset \mathcal{C}$. $\mathcal{C}_i^n \subset \mathcal{C}$ is the set of *neighboring cameras* of C_i and defined as all the cameras with which C_i is able to communicate. $\mathcal{C}_i^o \subset \mathcal{C}$ is the set of *overlapping cameras* of C_i, and is defined as all the cameras with which C_i can *potentially* have an overlapping field of view. (Adapted from [Song et al., 2010b])

overlapping field of view. By definition, it becomes clear then that for each $C_i \in \mathcal{C}_j^v$, it is true that $\mathcal{C}_j^v \subset \{\mathcal{C}_i^o \cup C_i\}$. We define $\mathcal{C}_i^c \subset \mathcal{C}$ as the connected component that C_i is in. We assume $\mathcal{C}_i^o \subset \mathcal{C}_i^c$, that is to say, C_i is able to exchange information with its overlapping cameras directly or via other cameras. A diagrammatic explanation of the notation is given in Figure 3.1.

We consider the situation where targets are moving on a ground plane and a homography between each camera's image plane and the ground plane is known. We will show how the state estimation for each target by each camera (i.e., each camera's estimates based on its individual measurements) can be combined together through the consensus scheme. This method is independent of the tracking scheme employed in each camera. If the network of cameras is connected, then consensus is achieved across the entire network.

3.3.2   EXTENDED KALMAN-CONSENSUS FILTER FOR A SINGLE TARGET

The Extended Kalman-Consensus filter allows us to track targets on the ground plane using multiple measurements in the image plane taken from various cameras. This allows each camera C_i to have at any time step k, a consensus state estimate $\bar{\mathbf{x}}_i^j$ and estimate error covariance $\mathbf{P}_i^j$ for each target T_j. To model the motion of a target T_j on the ground plane, we consider a linear discrete time dynamical system

$$\mathbf{x}^j(k+1) = \mathbf{A}^j(k)\mathbf{x}^j(k) + \mathbf{B}^j(k)\mathbf{w}^j(k), \quad \mathbf{x}^j(0) \sim \mathcal{N}(\mu_i^j, \mathbf{P}_0^j), \tag{3.1}$$

and nonlinear observation model for each camera C_i,

$$\mathbf{z}_i^j(k) = h_i(\mathbf{x}^j(k)) + \mathbf{v}_i^j(k), \tag{3.2}$$

where $h_i(.)$ is the mapping from the ground to the image plane for camera C_i, $\mathbf{w}^j(k)$ and $\mathbf{v}_i^j(k)$ are zero mean white Gaussian noise ($\mathbf{w}^j(k) \sim \mathcal{N}(0, \mathbf{Q}^j)$, $\mathbf{v}_i^j(k) \sim \mathcal{N}(0, \mathbf{R}_i^j)$) and $\mathbf{x}^j(0)$ is the initial state of the target. We define the state of the jth target at time step k as $\mathbf{x}^j(k) = (x^j(k), y^j(k), \dot{x}^j(k), \dot{y}^j(k))^T$ where $(x^j(k), y^j(k))$ and $(\dot{x}^j(k), \dot{y}^j(k))$ are the position and velocity of target T_j in the x and y directions respectively. The estimate state $\hat{\mathbf{x}}_i^j$ of T_j is based on the observations by the cameras viewing T_j. The noisy measurement $\mathbf{z}_i^j(k)$ at camera C_i is the sensed target position $(^{im}x_i^j(k), ^{im}y_i^j(k))$ on C_i's image plane.

Due to the nonlinear nature of the observation model, the linear Kalman-Consensus filter proposed in [Olfati-Saber and Sandell, 2008] cannot be applied as is. An extension to deal with the non-linearity of the observation model is required. Taking into account the nonlinear nature of our dynamical model, we propose an Extended Kalman-Consensus distributed tracking algorithm on the basis of the Kalman-Consensus filter detailed in [Olfati-Saber and Sandell, 2008]. The following are our basic Kalman filter iterations, as implemented in each camera, in the information form [1]:

• Prediction

$$\begin{aligned}
\mathbf{P}(k+1) &= \mathbf{A}(k)\mathbf{M}(k)\mathbf{A}(k)^T + \mathbf{B}(k)\mathbf{Q}(k)\mathbf{B}(k)^T, \\
\bar{\mathbf{x}}(k+1) &= \mathbf{A}(k)\hat{\mathbf{x}}(k).
\end{aligned} \tag{3.3}$$

• Correction

$$\begin{aligned}
\mathbf{M}(k)^{-1} &= \mathbf{P}(k)^{-1} + \mathbf{H}(k)^T\mathbf{R}(k)^{-1}\mathbf{H}(k), \\
\mathbf{K}(k) &= \mathbf{M}(k)\mathbf{H}(k)^T\mathbf{R}(k)^{-1}, \\
\hat{\mathbf{x}}(k) &= \bar{\mathbf{x}}(k) + \mathbf{K}(k)(\mathbf{z}(k) - h(\bar{\mathbf{x}}(k))).
\end{aligned} \tag{3.4}$$

Here, $\mathbf{P}$ and $\mathbf{M}$ are the *a priori* and *a posteriori* estimate error covariance matrix, respectively, and $\mathbf{H}$ is the Jacobian matrix of partial derivatives of h with respect to $\mathbf{x}$, i.e.,

$$\mathbf{H}_{[m,n]} = \frac{\partial h_{[m]}}{\partial \mathbf{x}_{[n]}}\bigg|_{\mathbf{x} = \bar{\mathbf{x}}(k)}. \tag{3.5}$$

This algorithm is performed at each camera node C_i. At each time step k and for each target T_j, we assume that we are given the estimated prior target state $\bar{\mathbf{x}}_i^j(k)$ and the error covariance matrix $\mathbf{P}_i^j$. At time step $k = 0$, the Extended Kalman-Consensus filter is initialized with $\mathbf{P}_i^j = \mathbf{P}_0$ and $\bar{\mathbf{x}}_i^j = E\langle \mathbf{x}_i^j(0)\rangle$. The consensus algorithm is shown in Algorithm 1.

The consensus process (Algorithm 1) is performed at each C_i for each T_j that is in the scene viewed by the camera network. $\mathcal{C}_i^n$ is the neighboring camera set of C_i and defined as all cameras

---

[1]The subscript/superscript that indicate camera/target is dropped here for ease of reading.

Algorithm 1 Distributed Extended Kalman-Consensus tracking algorithm performed by every C_i at discrete time step k. The state of T_j is represented by $\mathbf{x}_i^j$ with error covariance matrix $\mathbf{P}_i^j$.

Input: $\bar{\mathbf{x}}_i^j$ and $\mathbf{P}_i^j$ from time step $k-1$
for each T_j **do**

Obtain measurement $\mathbf{z}_i^j$ with covariance $\mathbf{R}_i^j$

Calculate Jacobian matrix $\mathbf{H}_i^j$ with respect to the observation model

$$(\mathbf{H}_i^j)_{[m,n]} = \left.\frac{\partial (h_i)_{[m]}}{\partial \mathbf{x}_{[n]}}\right|_{\mathbf{x}=\bar{\mathbf{x}}_i^j}$$

Compute information vector and matrix

$$\mathbf{u}_i^j = \mathbf{H}_i^{j^T} \mathbf{R}_i^{j-1} \mathbf{z}_i^j \text{ and } \mathbf{U}_i^j = \mathbf{H}_i^{j^T} \mathbf{R}_i^{j-1} \mathbf{H}_i^j$$

Compute the predicted measurement

$$\mathbf{g}_i^j = \mathbf{H}_i^{j^T} \mathbf{R}_i^{j-1} h_i(\bar{\mathbf{x}}_i^j)$$

Compute the residue

$$\mathbf{r}_i^j = \mathbf{u}_i^j - \mathbf{g}_i^j$$

Send message $\mathbf{m}_i^j = (\mathbf{r}_i^j, \mathbf{U}_i^j, \bar{\mathbf{x}}_i^j)$ to neighboring cameras $\mathcal{C}_i^n$
Receive messages $\mathbf{m}_l = (\mathbf{r}_l^j, \mathbf{U}_l^j, \bar{\mathbf{x}}_l^j)$ from all cameras $C_l \in \mathcal{C}_i^n$
Fuse information

$$\mathbf{y}_i^j = \sum_{l \in (C_i \cup \mathcal{C}_i^n)} \mathbf{r}_l^j, \ \mathbf{S}_i^j = \sum_{l \in (C_i \cup \mathcal{C}_i^n)} \mathbf{U}_l^j$$

Compute the Extend Kalman-Consensus state estimate

$$\mathbf{M}_i^j = ((\mathbf{P}_i^j)^{-1} + \mathbf{S}_i^j)^{-1} \tag{3.6}$$

$$\hat{\mathbf{x}}_i^j = \bar{\mathbf{x}}_i^j + \mathbf{M}_i^j \mathbf{y}_i^j + \gamma \mathbf{M}_i^j \sum_{l \in \mathcal{C}_i^n} (\bar{\mathbf{x}}_i^j - \bar{\mathbf{x}}_i^j) \tag{3.7}$$

$$\gamma = \epsilon/(\|\mathbf{M}_i^j\| + 1), \|\mathbf{X}\| = (tr(\mathbf{X}^T\mathbf{X}))^{\frac{1}{2}}$$

Update the state and error covariance matrix for time step k

$$\mathbf{P}_i^j \leftarrow \mathbf{A}^j \mathbf{M}_i^j \mathbf{A}^{j^T} + \mathbf{B}^j \mathbf{Q}^j \mathbf{B}^{j^T} \tag{3.8}$$

$$\bar{\mathbf{x}}_i^j \leftarrow \mathbf{A}^j \hat{\mathbf{x}}_i^j$$

end for

---

with which C_i can directly communicate. If C_i is viewing a target T_j, it obtains T_j's position on its image plane $\mathbf{z}_i^j$, and calculates the Jacobian matrix $\mathbf{H}_i^j$ of its observation model and consensus state estimate $\bar{\mathbf{x}}_i^j$. After that, the corresponding information vector $\mathbf{u}_i^j$ and matrix $\mathbf{U}_i^j$ are computed with the given measurement covariance matrix $\mathbf{R}_i^j$ and $\mathbf{H}_i^j$. Next, the predicted measurement $\mathbf{g}_i^j$ and corresponding residue $\mathbf{r}_i^j$ are calculated. C_i then sends a message $\mathbf{m}_i^j$ to its neighbors which includes the computed information matrix, residue and its estimated target state $\bar{\mathbf{x}}_i^j$ at previous time step $(k-1)$. Similar to [Olfati-Saber and Sandell, 2008], we define the information matrix and vector of $C_i \in \mathcal{C}_j^{v-}$ as $\mathbf{U}_i^j = 0$ and $\mathbf{u}_i^j = 0$ by assuming that their output matrices are zero, i.e., $\mathbf{H}_i^j = 0$ for all $C_i \in \mathcal{C}_j^{v-}$ to avoid any ambiguity arising from the lack of measurements in these cameras. C_i then receives similar messages $\mathbf{m}_l$ from the cameras in its neighborhood. The information matrices and residues received from these messages are then fused by C_i with its own information matrix and residue and the Extended Kalman-Consensus state estimate is computed. Finally, the ground plane state $\bar{\mathbf{x}}_i^j$ and error covariance matrix $\mathbf{P}_i^j$ are updated according to the assumed linear dynamical system.

3.3.3 JPDA-EKCF FOR TRACKING MULTIPLE TARGETS

One of fundamental problems for tracking multiple targets through an area monitored by multiple cameras is data association. This includes two tasks: the first task is the intra-camera data association, i.e., associating measurements observed by a camera to the targets; the second task is the inter-camera data association, i.e., establishing an association of estimated tracks between a camera and its neighbors. Next, we show how to deal with these two issues for tracking multiple targets in a distributed framework.

Intra-Camera Association

Due to fragility of low-level video processing methods, the image plane measurements are often noisy and there might be more measurements than the actual number of targets. Some targets may not be detected because of occlusion or appearance similar to the background. A direct one-to-one measurement-target assignment can lead to poor performance. The possibility of a false assignment and missed target detection should be considered.

As introduced in Chapter 2, Joint Probability Data Association (JPDA) [Bar-Shalom and Fortmann, 1988] computes an estimate over the various possibilities of measurement-to-track associations. Assume that at time step k, there are N_T targets in the scene and camera C_i obtains $N_M^i(k)$ measurements, $\mathbf{Z}_i(k) = \{\mathbf{z}_i^1(k), \ldots, \mathbf{z}_i^{N_M^i}(k)\}$. The history of measurements at camera C_i is denoted as $\mathcal{Z}_i(k) = \{\mathbf{Z}_i(1), \ldots, \mathbf{Z}_i(k)\}$. Let $\mathbf{x}^j$ denote the state of target T_j. Its *a posteriori* state estimate and *a prior* state estimate by camera C_i are denoted as $\hat{\mathbf{x}}_i^j$

and $\bar{\mathbf{x}}_i^j$, respectively. The state estimate of target T_j at camera C_i is

$$\hat{\mathbf{x}}_i^j = E[\mathbf{x}^j | \mathcal{Z}_i] = \sum_{n=1}^{N_M^i} E[\mathbf{x}^j | \chi_i^{jn}, \mathcal{Z}_i] P(\chi_i^{jn} | \mathcal{Z}_i) ,$$

where χ_i^{jn} denotes the event that measurement $\mathbf{z}_i^n$ associates to target T_j at camera C_i.

As an extension to standard Joint Probability Data Association Filter (JPDAF) [Bar-Shalom et al., 1980], the Extended Kalman Filter can be used to estimate $E[\mathbf{x}^j | \chi_i^{jn}, \mathcal{Z}_i]$. Let us denote $\beta_i^{jn} = P(\chi_i^{jn} | \mathcal{Z}_i)$ and $\beta_i^{j0} = 1 - \sum_{n=1}^{N_M^i} \beta_i^{jn}$ to represent the probability that target T_j has no measurement associated with it. Then the state estimate can be written as

$$\begin{aligned}
\hat{\mathbf{x}}_i^j &= \beta_i^{j0} \bar{\mathbf{x}}_i^j + \sum_{n=1}^{N_M^i} \beta_i^{jn} (\bar{\mathbf{x}}_i^j + \mathbf{K}_i^j (\mathbf{z}_i^n - h_i(\bar{\mathbf{x}}_i^j))) \\
&= \bar{\mathbf{x}}_i^j + \mathbf{K}_i^j \left(\sum_{n=1}^{N_M^i} \beta_i^{jn} \mathbf{z}_i^n - (1 - \beta_i^{j0}) h_i(\bar{\mathbf{x}}_i^j) \right) \\
&= \bar{\mathbf{x}}_i^j + \mathbf{K}_i^j \left(\tilde{\mathbf{z}}_i^j - (1 - \beta_i^{j0}) h_i(\bar{\mathbf{x}}_i^j) \right) ,
\end{aligned} \tag{3.9}$$

where

$$\tilde{\mathbf{z}}_i^j = \sum_{n=1}^{N_M^i} \beta_i^{jn} \mathbf{z}_i^n ,$$

and

$$\mathbf{K}_i^j = \mathbf{P}_i^j \mathbf{H}_i^{j^T} (\mathbf{H}_i^j \mathbf{P}_i^j \mathbf{H}_i^{j^T} + \mathbf{R}_i)^{-1} = \mathbf{P}_i^j \mathbf{H}_i^{j^T} (\mathbf{W}_i^j)^{-1} .$$

$\mathbf{H}_i^j$ is the Jacobian matrix of partial derivatives of h_i with respect to $\mathbf{x}_i^j$. The error covariance of the estimate is given by

$$\mathbf{M}_i^j = \mathbf{P}_i^j - (1 - \beta_i^{j0}) \mathbf{K}_i^j \mathbf{W}_i^j (\mathbf{K}_i^j)^T + \mathbf{K}_i^j \tilde{\mathbf{P}}_i^j (\mathbf{K}_i^j)^T ,$$

where

$$\tilde{\mathbf{P}}_i^j = \sum_{n=1}^{N_M^i} \beta_i^{jn} (\mathbf{z}_i^n - h_i(\bar{\mathbf{x}}_i^j))(\mathbf{z}_i^n - h_i(\bar{\mathbf{x}}_i^j))^T - (\tilde{\mathbf{z}}_i^j - h_i(\bar{\mathbf{x}}_i^j))(\tilde{\mathbf{z}}_i^j - h_i(\bar{\mathbf{x}}_i^j))^T .$$

While tracking target in clutter, validation gates are usually used to filter out measurements from clutter within the environment. A validation gate is a metric of "acceptability", i.e., within the gate, it is treated as a valid measurement, otherwise it is rejected. Let P_D be the probability that the correct measurement is detected, and P_G be the probability that the correct measurement, if detected, lies within the gate. As shown in [Fortmann et al., 1983], by assuming a Poisson distribution for false measurements lying in the gate and a Gaussian distribution for associating a measurement with a target, using Bayes' rule, the β_i^j's can be calculated as:

$$\beta_i^{jn} = \frac{\exp\left(-(\mathbf{v}_i^{jn})^T \Lambda^{-1} \mathbf{v}_i^{jn}/2\right)}{b + \sum_{n=1}^{N_M^i} \exp\left(-(\mathbf{v}_i^{jn})^T \Lambda^{-1} \mathbf{v}_i^{jn}/2\right)}$$

$$\beta_i^{j0} = \frac{b}{b + \sum_{n=1}^{N_M^i} \exp\left(-(\mathbf{v}_i^{jn})^T \Lambda^{-1} \mathbf{v}_i^{jn}/2\right)}$$

$$b = (2\pi)^{d/2} \lambda_f \det(\Lambda)^{1/2} (1 - P_D P_G)/P_D,$$

where $\mathbf{v}_i^{jn} = \mathbf{z}_i^n - h_i(\bar{\mathbf{x}}_i^j)$, Λ is the covariance of the distribution of $\mathbf{v}$, d is the dimension of measurement vector and λ_f is the expected number of occurrences of the Poisson distribution.

Inter-Camera Association

In distributed tracking of multiple targets, each camera has its own set of estimated tracks and also receives track estimates from its neighbors. Therefore, it is necessary to establish an association between these tracks. This can be formulated as a maximum matching problem in a weighted bipartite graph [Javed et al., 2003] which minimizes the matching cost. The Hungarian algorithm [Kuhn, 1955] can be used to find the maximum matching. Different distance metrics can be used to find the matching cost between two track estimates from different cameras. For example, the Mahalanobis distance metric gives distance measures by incorporating covariance information, i.e.,

$$D(\bar{\mathbf{x}}_i^j, \bar{\mathbf{x}}_{i'}^{j'}) = (\bar{\mathbf{x}}_i^j - \bar{\mathbf{x}}_{i'}^{j'})^T (\mathbf{P}_i^j + \mathbf{P}_{i'}^{j'})^{-1} (\bar{\mathbf{x}}_i^j - \bar{\mathbf{x}}_{i'}^{j'}).$$

JPDA-EKCF algorithm

We now show that distributed multiple target tracking can be achieved by integrating data association with a distributed single target tracker. In [Sandell and Olfati-Saber, 2008], Joint Probability Data Association (JPDA) is coupled with Kalman-Consensus Filter (KCF) estimator, where JPDA is used to perform local measurement-to-track associations. This algorithm is referred as JPDA-KCF. Due to the nonlinear nature of the observation model in the camera network, an extension to deal with the non-linearity is required. Here, we describe an Extended Kalman-Consensus Filter coupled with Joint Probability Data Association along the lines of the JPDA-KCF detailed in [Sandell and Olfati-Saber, 2008]. The entire process is shown in Algorithm 2.

The JPDA-EKCF algorithm is performed at each C_i for each T_j that is in the scene under surveillance, where C_i^n is the neighboring camera set of C_i and defined as all cameras with which C_i can directly communicate. Camera C_i computes the assignment of the measurements to targets using JPDA. Then C_i calculates the Jacobian matrix $\mathbf{H}_i^j$ of its observation model with respect to the consensus state estimate $\bar{\mathbf{x}}_i^j$ of last time step. After that, the corresponding information vector $\mathbf{u}_i^j$ and matrix $\mathbf{U}_i^j$ are computed with the given measurement covariance matrix $\mathbf{R}_i^j$ and $\mathbf{H}_i^j$. Next,

Algorithm 2 JPDA-EKCF algorithm performed by every C_i at discrete time step k. The state of T_j is represented by $\mathbf{x}_i^j$ with error covariance matrix $\mathbf{P}_i^j$.

Input: $\bar{\mathbf{x}}_i^j$ and $\mathbf{P}_i^j$ from time step $k-1$
Obtain measurement set $\mathbf{Z}_i = \{\mathbf{z}_i^n\}$ with covariances $\{\mathbf{R}_i\}$.

Use JPDA to compute the weights β_i^{jn}.

Calculate Jacobian matrix $\mathbf{H}_i^j$ with respect to the observation model

$$(\mathbf{H}_i^j)_{[m,n]} = \frac{\partial(h_i)_{[m]}}{\partial\mathbf{x}_{[n]}}\bigg|_{\mathbf{x}=\bar{\mathbf{x}}_i^j}.$$

Compute information vector and matrix

$$\mathbf{u}_i^j = \mathbf{H}_i^{j^T}\mathbf{R}_i^{-1}\sum_{n=1}^{N_M^i}\beta_i^{jn}\mathbf{z}_i^n \text{ and } \mathbf{U}_i^j = \mathbf{H}_i^{j^T}\mathbf{R}_i^{-1}\mathbf{H}_i^j.$$

Compute the predicted measurement

$$\mathbf{g}_i^j = \mathbf{H}_i^{j^T}\mathbf{R}_i^{-1}h_i(\bar{\mathbf{x}}_i^j).$$

Compute the residue

$$\mathbf{r}_i^j = \mathbf{u}_i^j - (1-\beta_i^{j0})\mathbf{g}_i^j.$$

Send message $\mathcal{M}_i$ to neighboring cameras $\mathcal{C}_i^n$, $\mathcal{M}_i$ contains

    1. $(\mathbf{r}_i^1, \mathbf{r}_i^2, \ldots, \mathbf{r}_i^{N_T})$.   2. $(\mathbf{U}_i^1, \mathbf{U}_i^2, \ldots, \mathbf{U}_i^{N_T})$,
    3. $(\bar{\mathbf{x}}_i^1, \bar{\mathbf{x}}_i^2, \ldots, \bar{\mathbf{x}}_i^{N_T})$,   4. $(\mathbf{P}_i^1, \mathbf{P}_i^2, \ldots, \mathbf{P}_i^{N_T})$.

Receive messages $\mathcal{M}_l$ from all cameras $C_l \in \mathcal{C}_i^n$.
Compute inter-camera track-to-track matchings g_{il}.
Fuse information

$$\mathbf{y}_i^j = \sum_{l\in(C_i\cup\mathcal{C}_i^n)}\mathbf{r}_l^{g_{il}(j)}, \quad \mathbf{S}_i^j = \sum_{l\in(C_i\cup\mathcal{C}_i^n)}\mathbf{U}_l^{g_{il}(j)}.$$

Compute the Extend Kalman-Consensus state estimate

$$\hat{\mathbf{x}}_i^j = \bar{\mathbf{x}}_i^j + \left((\mathbf{P}_i^j)^{-1}+\mathbf{S}_i^j\right)^{-1}\mathbf{y}_i^j + \gamma\mathbf{M}_i^j\sum_{l\in\mathcal{C}_i^n}(\bar{\mathbf{x}}_l^{g_{il}(j)}-\bar{\mathbf{x}}_i^j),$$

$$\gamma = \epsilon/(||\mathbf{M}_i^j||+1), ||\mathbf{X}|| = (tr(\mathbf{X}^T\mathbf{X}))^{\frac{1}{2}},$$

$$\mathbf{M}_i^j = \beta_i^{j0}\mathbf{P}_i^j + (1-\beta_i^{j0})\left((\mathbf{P}_i^j)^{-1}+\mathbf{S}_i^j\right)^{-1} + \mathbf{K}_i^j\tilde{\mathbf{P}}_i^j(\mathbf{K}_i^j)^T.$$

Update the state and error covariance matrix for time step k

$$\mathbf{P}_i^j \leftarrow \mathbf{A}^j\mathbf{M}_i^j\mathbf{A}^{j^T} + \mathbf{B}^j\mathbf{Q}^j\mathbf{B}^{j^T},$$

$$\bar{\mathbf{x}}_i^j \leftarrow \mathbf{A}^j\hat{\mathbf{x}}_i^j.$$

predicted measurements and its corresponding residues are calculated. C_i then sends a message $\mathcal{M}_i$ to its neighbors which includes the computed information matrices, residues and its estimated target state $\bar{\mathbf{x}}_i^j$ and error covariance $\mathbf{P}_i^j$ at previous time step $(k-1)$. C_i then receives similar messages $\mathcal{M}_l$ only from the cameras in its neighborhood. Based on the received information, C_i finds the inter-camera track-to-track matchings. The information matrices and residues received from these messages are then fused by C_i with its own information matrices and residues according to the cross camera track matching results and the Extended Kalman-Consensus state estimate is computed. Finally, the ground plane state $\bar{\mathbf{x}}_i^j$ and error covariance matrix $\mathbf{P}_i^j$ are updated according to the assumed linear dynamical system.

3.3.4   HANDOFF IN CONSENSUS TRACKING ALGORITHMS

For wide-area tracking algorithms, it is necessary to develop suitable handoff strategies between the cameras. Through the Kalman-consensus algorithm, each C_i has a consensus-based ground plane state estimate of each target that is being viewed by the cameras with which C_i can exchange information directly or indirectly, even if C_i has never seen some of the targets. For the case of overlapping cameras, a target T_j visible in camera C_i's FOV will also be visible in the FOV of an overlapping camera $C_{i'} \in C_i^o$. C_i can exchange information with its overlapping cameras, C_i^o, directly or via other cameras. Therefore, $C_{i'}$ can track T_j and find the target correspondence in a seamless way since it had knowledge of T_j's ground plane position through the consensus-tracking. If the target moves from one camera to another that is non-overlapping, the distributed data association strategies outlined above can be employed to find the correspondences and maintain the continuity of the track.

Another advantage of the fact that cameras have knowledge of all the targets in their neighborhood is that in the event of a sudden failure of camera node C_i, the targets that were viewed by C_i are not suddenly lost by the camera network. Also, a camera may take a short amount of time to change its parameters to a new position in a non-static camera network. If no camera is viewing the target for the short amount of time it takes for the cameras to come to a new set of parameters, the target state estimate and covariance continue to propagate. This does not translate to a significant decrease in tracking performance as seen in our experiments.

3.3.5   EXAMPLE OF DISTRIBUTED TRACKING USING EKCF

We now show some experimental results on implementing the above consensus algorithms. Tracking results are shown in a real camera network composed of 10 PTZ cameras looking over an outdoor area of approximately 10000 sq. feet. In the area under surveillance, there were 8 targets in total. Figure 3.2 shows the tracking results as viewed by each camera at 4 time instants.

The results are shown on a non-static camera network. The cameras are controlled to always cover the entire area under surveillance through a game theoretic control framework proposed in [Soto et al., 2009]. The change of camera settings does not affect the procedure of the EKCF. Figure 3.2(a) shows the initial settings of the camera network that covers the entire area. As the

(a) $k = 64$

(b) $k = 84$

(c) $k = 90$

(d) $k = 138$

Figure 3.2: Each sub-figure shows 10 cameras at one of four time instants denoted by k. The track of one target, marked with a box, is shown. All targets are tracked using the Kalman-Consensus filtering approach, but are not marked for clarity. (From [Song et al., 2010b])

targets are observed in this area, the single-view tracking module in each camera determines the ground plane position of each target in its FOV and sends that information to the Kalman-Consensus filter which processes it together with the information received from the Kalman-Consensus filters of neighboring cameras as described in Section 3.3.3.

Figure 3.2(b) shows the instant when a camera C_6 is focused on a target T_1^h. Figures 3.2(b) and (c) show the dynamics of the targets in the camera network. All targets are tracked using the Kalman-consensus scheme, although we show the marked track for only one target. The handoff of T_1^h is clearly shown in Figure 3.2(d) from C_6 to C_3. It is to be noted that every time a target goes from one camera's FOV into another one, or when a camera changes its parameters, the network topologies for the targets, i.e., C_l^v and C_l^{v-}, also change.

Figure 3.3(a) shows the distributed Kalman-Consensus tracks for the 8 targets. The measurements of the different cameras are shown in a light gray color. As can be seen, the Kalman-Consensus filter in each camera comes to a smooth estimate of the actual state for each target.

Figure 3.3(b) shows the distributed tracking results on the ground plane for one of the targets, T_5. The dots correspond to the ground plane measurements from different cameras viewing the target while the solid line is the consensus-based estimate. As can be expected, the individual positions are different for each camera due to calibration and single-view tracking inaccuracies. As can be seen clearly, even though C_5^v is time varying, the Kalman-Consensus filter estimates the target's position seamlessly at all times.

In Figure 3.3(a) and (b), the cameras that are viewing the same target can communicate with each other directly, i.e., $\forall l$, C_l^v is a fully connected graph. The results are exactly the same as a centralized case similar to each cluster of [Medeiros et al., 2008]. We denote the results of this fully connected case as KCF1. In order to show the effect of the network communication topology on the Kalman-consensus tracking, we consider an example of a partially connected network, which is shown on the right-top of Figure 3.3(c). Compared to the fully connected one, direct communication does not exist either between camera 1 and camera 3, or between camera 4 and camera 8. Figure 3.3(c) shows the KCF tracking results at Camera 1 for this case, which is denoted as KCF2. It is slightly different from KCF1, due to the difference in the fused information.

The consensus method is guaranteed to have the same result as the centralized case if there are no limitations on the communication capabilities. In the case of partial connection between cameras, KCF will converge to the centralized result as the number of consensus iterations goes to infinity [Olfati-Saber, 2007]. However, the limited communication will result in differences from the centralized result for a finite number of steps (as shown in Figure 3.3(c)). However, even in this case, the consensus result is better than that obtained at each individual camera, as shown in Figure 3.3(d) and explained below.

In order to measure tracking performance, we compare the tracking results with the groundtruth trajectory, which is shown in Figure 3.3(c). In the table at the bottom, we show the minimum, maximum and average distances to the groundtruth of KCF1, KCF2 and individual camera tracks. It can be seen that KCF1 performs best and KCF2 is better than individual camera tracks.

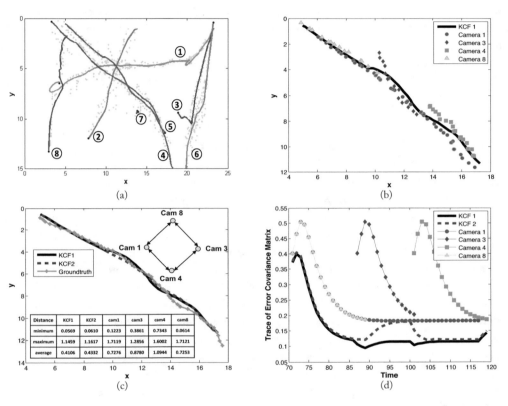

Figure 3.3: Tracking results. (a) Distributed Kalman-Consensus tracking trajectories for 8 targets. Measurements from all cameras are shown in a light gray color. (b) Tracking results on the ground plane for one of the targets T_5. cameras that are viewing the same target can communicate with each other directly, i.e., $\forall l$, $\mathcal{C}_l^v$ is a fully connected graph. The results are exactly same as centralized case. We denote the results of this full connection as KCF1. (c) KCF tracking results at Camera 1 given an example of a partially connected camera network, which is shown on the top-right. This case is denoted as KCF2. We can see that Cam (1,3) and Cam (4,8) cannot communicate. The groundtruth trajectory is also marked. The comparison of tracking performances (minimum, maximum and average distances to the groundtruth) of KCF1, KCF2 and individual camera tracks are shown in the table at the bottom. (d) Trace of the error covariance of the tracking results for the same target shown in (b) and (c). (From [Song et al., 2010b])

We also look at the output error covariance matrix $\mathbf{P}$ of the Kalman filter. The higher the trace of $\mathbf{P}$ is, the lower the tracking accuracy is. Figure 3.3(d) shows the traces of the covariance matrix of the tracking error for the same target as in Figure 3.3(b) and (c). The colored lines with symbols correspond to tracking results from different cameras using their own measurements only (as each camera runs an independent Kalman filter), while the solid black line is the result of consensus-based estimate for the fully connected case (which will be the same for the centralized case) and dashed purple line is for the partially connected one. As can be seen clearly, the Kalman-Consensus filter with full connection performs the best, and the partially connected one does better than individual Kalman filters without consensus.

3.3.6   SPARSE NETWORKS AND NAIVE NODES - THE GENERALIZED KALMAN CONSENSUS FILTER

The KCF is a very appropriate framework for camera networks and has been applied in [Song et al., 2011a, 2010b]. The KCF algorithm works under the assumption that all the sensors have sensed all the targets. However, certain issues that are specific to video sensors have not been considered. A camera is a unidirectional sensor with a limited sensing region which is called the field-of-view (FOV). Thus, in a realistic camera network, a target would usually be seen in only a few of the nodes. In a distributed decision making process, the nodes are assumed to have peer-to-peer communication channels. Thus, when a sensor gets new measurements for a target, say T_j, it shares this measurement information with its network neighbors. This measurement information is used to update the estimate of T_j's state and error covariance at each node that directly observes T_j or receives measurement of T_j from their neighbor(s). At the same time, the nodes also share their previous state estimate with each other and try to compensate the difference between their state estimates of T_j using a consensus scheme. Thus, at some nodes in the network that are neither sensing T_j directly nor are neighbor to a node sensing T_j (termed as *naive nodes* for T_j), the state estimate for this target is only adjusted by the consensus scheme and its error covariance is not adjusted; therefore, the error covariance matrices of each target may diverge.

Such issues are important for networks with sparse communication topology. For example, camera networks are often spread over a wide area which prevents each camera from communicating with all other cameras. There can be many naive nodes in sparse communication topologies.

Definition: Naive Node. In a realistic camera network a node might exist where neither the node C_i nor its immediate neighbors $C_{i'}, i' \in N_{C_i}$ can see a specific target T_j. In this particular scenario, C_i is naive about T_j in the sense that it cannot *directly* receive any observation update about T_j. We call such a node C_i, '*Naive*' relative to target T_j.

The presence of these naive nodes motivates us to propose certain modifications to the KCF framework – the Generalized Kalman Consensus Filter (GKCF) [Kamal et al., 2011]—for application in camera networks.

Motivation of GKCF

Now we discuss in detail various specific conditions that require attention when the KCF is applied to sparse (e.g., camera) networks with naive nodes, and to propose solution strategies for each of them.

1) Average vs. weighted average: The basic KCF algorithm uses *average* consensus to combine state estimates from neighboring nodes (see eqn. (3.7)). With average consensus, the state estimates of all the nodes get the same weight in the summation. Since naive nodes do not have observations of the target, their estimates are often highly erroneous. This results in reduced performance in the presence of naive nodes.

2) Covariance/Information Matrix Propagation: The covariance matrix measurement update of eqn. (3.6) considers the node's own covariance matrix and the local neighborhood's measurement covariance. It does not account for cross covariance between the estimates by the node and its neighbors. In the theoretical proof of optimality for KCF, the cross covariances terms between neighbors' state estimates were present [Olfati-Saber, 2009]. It has been stated in [Olfati-Saber, 2009] that dropping these cross covariance terms is a valid approximation when the state estimate error covariance matrices are almost equal in all the nodes.

However, when C_i is naive w.r.t. T_j, $\mathbf{y}_i$ and $\mathbf{S}_i$ are both zero. Therefore, $\mathbf{M}_i^j = (\mathbf{P}_i^j)$ at eqn. (3.6). Consequently, from eqn. (3.8) it can be seen that the covariance matrix diverge. From this, it can be clearly seen that omitting the cross covariances in the covariance update equation is not valid for sparse networks with naive agents. The correlation between the two dependent variables is the unknown parameter making this computation difficult. There has been some work, e.g. [Ren et al., 2005] and [Alighanbari and How, 2006], where the authors incorporated cross covariance information, which should lead to the optimum result. But, no method for computing these terms was provided and predefined fixed values were used instead.

3) State Update: The measurement update term and consensus term in eqn. (3.7) are both functions of the prior state estimate $\hat{\mathbf{x}}_i^-(k)$. Both terms apply corrections to the prior state estimate from different information sources. Without a proper weighting term between them, the state estimate may be incorrectly updated. This is usually not a big issue in sensor networks without naive nodes because every node's state estimate will be close to the consensus. In sparse networks, the estimates of naive nodes may lag behind by a significant time. This happens because naive nodes do not have direct access to new observation of a target, the only way they can get updated information about a target is through a neighbor's state estimate which was updated in the previous iteration. Thus, a naive node might be multiple iterations away from getting new information about a target. This information imbalance can cause large oscillations. In the KCF algorithms this effect can be decreased by choosing a smaller rate parameter ϵ. However, decreasing ϵ yields slower convergence of the naive node's state estimate.

The above issues can be problematic for tracking applications involving a camera network with naive nodes. A naive node may associate an observation to a wrong target. This can affect the tracking performance of nodes that are actually observing the target by influencing them to drift away from their estimates. Since KCF is a very appropriate framework to build a distributed tracker in a camera network, we propose some changes to address the above challenges leading to a Generalized Kalman Consensus Filter. The following are the main proposed modifications.

1) The consensus portion of the GKCF correction step at each node will take into account the state covariances of neighbors. The nodes will then converge towards the weighted mean, instead the unweighted mean.

2) Each node and its neighbors' state covariance matrices will be used jointly at consensus step to update that node's error covariance matrix. This will prevent the state covariance of the naive nodes from monotonically increasing.

3) The consensus and measurement terms will be weighted properly leading to a more accurate state update.

Generalized Kalman Consensus Filter

The proposed GKCF approach is presented in Algorithm 3. To derive our approach in Algorithm 3, we first introduce the weighted average consensus. Next, we show how to incorporate this consensus scheme into our framework. We then implement the Distributed Kalman Filter (DKF) with the results from the weighted average consensus and show how to propagate our covariance and state estimates. For the purpose of easy representation, we use $\mathbf{W}$ to denote the information matrix, or inverse covariance matrix, i.e., $\mathbf{W}^{-1} = \mathbf{P}$. In this section, we will use $\mathbf{W}^{-1}$ to replace $\mathbf{P}$ as in sections 3.3.2 and 3.3.3.

Weighted Average Consensus

Let the initial state estimate of all N_C agents be $\mathbf{x}_i(0)$ with information matrix $\mathbf{W}_i(0)$. As we use this information matrix term as weights in the weighted average consensus algorithm, the terms *weight* and *information matrix* will be used interchangeably. Also, let $\mathbf{W}(0) = \sum_{i=1}^{N_C} \mathbf{W}_i(0)$. So, the global weighted average of the initial states is

$$\mathbf{x}^* = \mathbf{W}(0)^{-1} \sum_{i=1:N_C} \mathbf{W}_i(0)\mathbf{x}_i(0). \tag{3.10}$$

Define the weighted initial state of each agent as

$$\tilde{\mathbf{x}}_i(0) = \mathbf{W}_i(0)\mathbf{x}_i(0). \tag{3.11}$$

Weighted average consensus [Olfati-Saber et al., 2007] states that if the iterative update in Equations (3.15) and (3.16) is performed for all $i = 1, \ldots, N_c$, then each of the terms $\mathbf{W}_i(\kappa)^{-1}\tilde{\mathbf{x}}_i(\kappa)$ tends to the global weighted average $\mathbf{x}^*$ as $\kappa \to \infty$. As a by-product, the weights also converge to the average of the initial weights. Both these properties of the weighted average consensus will be utilized in our approach.

We assume that the initial information matrix $\mathbf{W}_i(0)$, is provided at the initial time step by the target detection mechanism. It would ideally be zero for nodes that are not detecting the target. For nodes that are detecting the target, the initial value would be $\mathbf{W}_i(k-1) = \mathbf{H}_i^\top \mathbf{R}^{-1} \mathbf{H}_i$.

Algorithm 3 Multi-target GKCF on sensor C_i

Given $\mathbf{W}_i^j(0), \hat{\mathbf{x}}_i^{j+}(0), \epsilon$ and K. Also let,

$$\tilde{\mathbf{x}}_i^j(0) = \mathbf{W}_i^j(0)\hat{\mathbf{x}}_i^{j+}(0) \tag{3.12}$$

for k = 1 to K **do**

1.   Get measurements $\{^i\mathbf{z}_l\}_{l=1}^L$

2.   Associate observations to targets using Hungarian Algorithm. Let the observation associated with T_j in C_i be $\mathbf{z}_i^j$. If no observation in associated, set $\mathbf{z}_i^j = \mathbf{0}$ and $(\mathbf{R}_i^j)^{-1} = \mathbf{0}$

3.   Compute information vector and matrix

$$\mathbf{u}_i^j = (\mathbf{H}_i^j)^T (\mathbf{R}_i^j)^{-1} \mathbf{z}_i^j \qquad \mathbf{U}_i^j = (\mathbf{H}_i^j)^T (\mathbf{R}_i^j)^{-1} \mathbf{H}_i^j \tag{3.13}$$

4.   Broadcast message $\mathcal{M}_i$ to neighbors containing
$\mathbf{u}_i^j, \mathbf{U}_i^j, \tilde{\mathbf{x}}_i^j(k-1), \mathbf{W}_i^j(k-1) \quad \forall j$

5.   Receive message $\mathcal{M}_{i'}$ from neighbors $C_{i'} \in \mathcal{C}_i^n$

6.   Compute inter-camera data association matchings using the method described in Section 3.3.3 (Inter-Camera Association) and sort all data accordingly.

7.   Fuse the information matrices and vectors

$$\mathbf{y}_i^j = \sum_{C_{i'} \in (C_i \cup \mathcal{C}_i^n)} \mathbf{u}_{i'}^j \qquad \mathbf{S}_i^j = \sum_{C_{i'} \in (C_i \cup \mathcal{C}_i^n)} \mathbf{U}_{i'}^j \tag{3.14}$$

8.   Compute weighted average consensus estimate

$$\tilde{\mathbf{x}}_i^j(k) = \tilde{\mathbf{x}}_i^j(k-1) + \epsilon \sum_{C_{i'} \in \mathcal{C}_i^n} \left(\tilde{\mathbf{x}}_{i'}^j(k-1) - \tilde{\mathbf{x}}_i^j(k-1)\right) \tag{3.15}$$

$$\mathbf{W}_i^j(k) = \mathbf{W}_i^j(k-1) + \epsilon \sum_{C_{i'} \in \mathcal{C}_i^n} \left(\mathbf{W}_{i'}^j(k-1) - \mathbf{W}_i^j(k-1)\right) \tag{3.16}$$

$$\hat{\mathbf{x}}_i^{j-}(k) = \mathbf{W}_i^j(k)^{-1} \tilde{\mathbf{x}}_i^j(k) \tag{3.17}$$

9.   Compute Kalman consensus estimate

$$\mathbf{W}_i^j(k) = \mathbf{W}_i^j(k) + \mathbf{S}_i^j \tag{3.18}$$

$$\hat{\mathbf{x}}_i^{j+}(k) = \hat{\mathbf{x}}_i^{j-}(k) + \mathbf{W}_i^j(k)^{-1} \left(\mathbf{y}_i^j - \mathbf{S}_i^j \hat{\mathbf{x}}_i^{j-}(k)\right) \tag{3.19}$$

10.   Propagate weight and weighted state estimate

$$\mathbf{W}_i^j(k) \leftarrow (\mathbf{A}\mathbf{W}_i^j(k)^{-1}\mathbf{A}^T + \mathbf{Q})^{-1} \tag{3.20}$$

$$\tilde{\mathbf{x}}_i^j(k) \leftarrow \mathbf{W}_i^j(k)\mathbf{A}\hat{\mathbf{x}}_i^{j+}(k) \tag{3.21}$$

end for

At the kth iteration, the agents communicate with each other with the $\mathbf{W}_i(k-1)$ and $\tilde{\mathbf{x}}_i(k-1)$ information. Then, using the previously discussed average consensus scheme, they get an updated prior state estimate $\hat{\mathbf{x}}_i^-(k)$ and weight estimate $\mathbf{W}_i(k)$ (see eqns. (3.15), (3.16) and (3.17)). This prior estimate tends towards the global normalized weighted average as stated before.

Covariance/Information Matrix Propagation   After communicating with its neighbors and prior to using measurement information, the optimal state estimate at C_i is a linear combination of the information from C_i and its neighbors. Since these variables are not independent, optimal estimation would require knowledge of the cross correlation structure between each pair of these random variables. Since, it is usually quite difficult to compute this cross correlation, we need some other way to approximate the covariance or in this case the information matrix. The update operation of the information matrix $\mathbf{W}_i(k)$ in eqn. (3.16) can be used as an approximation of the information matrix due to the incoming information from the neighbors' states. A property of the weighted average consensus is that the weights also converge to the average of the weights as the state estimates converge towards the weighted average. Thus, this kind of covariance/weight propagation enables the weights to be updated accordingly when informative state estimates arrive at a naive node.

After computing the state and weight estimates with all the available information, we need to propagate the weight and state in time. One should note that instead of propagating the state estimate, we have to propagate the weighted state estimate as necessitated by the weighted average consensus equations. Thus, the weight propagation equation takes the form of eqn. (3.20).

Weighted State Update   To describe the proper weighting between the consensus and innovation terms in the state update process, consider the estimation process in two stages. First, as mentioned above, C_i updates its state and information matrix using its neighbors' states and information matrices. Next, we further update our state and information matrix with current measurement information, which we explain below.

Consider that a node that has completed Step 3 in Algorithm 3. If it did not have any observation, then $\mathbf{z}_i$ and $(\mathbf{R}_i)^{-1}$ were set to zero. Using the fused information vector and matrix and the updated prior weight and state estimate (from the weighted average consensus step of eqns. (3.16) and (3.17)) appropriately, we get the final state and weight estimate at time k. Thus, using DKF in eqns. (3.18) and (3.19) we can estimate the state and weight which includes the properly weighted innovations from the measurements and the state estimates of the neighbors.

Note that in a more general algorithm, at the expense of additional communications, the weighted consensus of Step 8 could be performed multiple times between measurements. Then the state estimates would converge even closer to the global weighted average (by virtue of the weighted average consensus steps). Also note that the GKCF achieves its improved performance at the expense of additional communication, as it requires communication of the information matrix for each observed target whereas the KCF does not.

3.4 CAMERA NETWORK CALIBRATION

In this section, we review methods for distributed calibration of camera networks. Since calibration requires data association, we start with a description of this topic, followed by calibration methods. Thereafter, we show how 3D pose estimation can be done in a distributed environment once the calibration parameters are known.

3.4.1 DISTRIBUTED DATA ASSOCIATION

In distributed architectures, usually a network topology is considered where a camera node (camera) can only communicate with a node directly connected to it (neighboring node). The goal of a distributed approach for data association in camera networks is that the cameras must come to consensus only by communicating with their network neighbors and without sending all the information to each other or to a centralized server.

In initial work on camera networks, particular interest was focused on learning a network topology, i.e., configuring connections between cameras and entry/exit points in their view. This is critical for establishing associations between multiple views. The authors in [Rahimi and Darrell, 2004] used the location and velocity of objects moving across multiple non-overlapping cameras to estimate the calibration parameters of the cameras and the targets' trajectories. In [Markis et al., 2004], the links between camera views were learned by exploiting the statistical consistency of the observation data. A framework for handoff between cameras was described in [Javed et al., 2000] by finding the limits of the field of view (FOV) of one camera in other cameras. This method was adopted in [Wang et al., 2010b] with consideration of power and bandwidth constraints with wireless embedded smart-cameras.

A lot of effort has been devoted to studying data associations for multi-target tracking, but many challenges remain in their applicability to camera networks, especially in distributed environments. Multi-Hypothesis Tracking (MHT) [Reid, 1979] and Joint Probabilistic Data Association Filters (JPDAF) [Bar-Shalom and Fortmann, 1988] are two representative methods. In order to overcome the large computational cost of MHT and JPDAF, various optimization algorithms such as Linear Programming [Jiang et al., 2007], and Hungarian algorithm [Kuhn, 1955] are used for data association. In [Zhang et al., 2008], the authors proposed a min-cost flow framework for global optimal data association. There are a few papers on applying these techniques to camera networks with consideration of the geometrical relationship between cameras. In [Dixon et al., 2009], the data association across cameras is achieved by extending the min-cost flow algorithm to camera networks. However, the approach cannot be straightforwardly applied to distributed camera networks. An inter-camera matching method is presented in [Ermis et al., 2010] by exploiting geometrical independence properties. The authors also considered the communication efficiency aspect through compressive sensing which has the potential to be used in a distributed manner.

The problem of distributed data association has been addressed in [Chen et al., 2005, Sandell and Olfati-Saber, 2008]. In [Sandell and Olfati-Saber, 2008], a probabilistic data association technique called JPDA (Joint Probabilistic Data Association) was used. The system was initialized with the correct number of tracks. Then at each time step, each of the cameras updated the tracks with a probabilistic fusion of all its own observations. Next, they conveyed the tracks to their neighboring cameras and associated the closest tracks to each other. After this data association step, the associated tracks from neighboring cameras were fused together using a Kalman Consensus framework, as explained in detail in Chapter 3.3.3. In [Chen et al., 2005], a graphical method is used to solve the data association problem in a distributed framework. Virtual Nodes were assumed for each camera, target and non-overlapping region allowing distributed Message Passing Algorithms for graphical models to be used to solve the data association problem. These virtual nodes may be available in a centralized server or may be distributed among the cameras. The prior spatial distribution of the targets was assumed to be known by the cameras covering each particular region. Then by sharing the data association confidences with each other, all the nodes came to an agreement about the data association. The camera calibration was assumed to be known in both of these distributed data association papers.

The problem of distributed calibration of camera networks has also garnered some interest in recent years. Average consensus based methods as in [Elhamifar and Vidal, 2009], and graphical methods as in [Devarajan and Radke, 2007], have been used to estimate calibration parameters in a distributed manner. However, these solutions for the calibration parameters require reliable data association to be available at each of the nodes. From the above discussion, we can see that distributed data association and calibration are closely inter-linked. We are not familiar with any work yet in distributed camera networks that looks at these two problems jointly and it is a very interesting topic for future research.

3.4.2   DISTRIBUTED CALIBRATION

Camera calibration consists in the estimation of a model for an un-calibrated camera. The objective is to find the external parameters (position and orientation relatively to a world coordinate system), and the internal parameters of the camera (principal point or image center, focal length and distortion coefficients). Single camera calibration has been extensively studied [Tsai, 1986, Zhang, 2000]. These methods usually involve a calibration pattern, and find the camera parameters by minimizing the re-projection error between the two-dimensional(2-D) projections of known 3-D points in the pattern and their measured 2-D projections in the image. The methods for single camera calibration may not scale well for large camera networks and independent calibration of each camera cannot guarantee global consistency.

Self-Calibration methods [Hartley, 1994, Maybank and Faugeras, 1992, Pollefeys et al., 1999, Triggs, 1997], on the other hand, make few assumptions about the particular structure of the scene being viewed. Calibration can be accomplished by minimizing a nonlinear cost function of the calibration parameters and a collection of unknown 3-D scene points projecting to matched image correspondences. This problem is also known as Structure from Motion (SFM) and is a highly non-linear problem. Good results are achievable when the image correspondences can be computed reliably. However, within the scope of this chapter, we will focus on calibration in distributed camera networks.

Calibration based on a known object is a common method; for example, in [Barton-Sweeney et al., 2006], a light-weight protocol for camera calibration is proposed. The part of the network contains wireless nodes equipped with CMOS camera modules, while the rest of the nodes are equipped with unique modulated LED emissions in order to uniquely identify themselves to the cameras. An Extended Kalman Filtering framework is implemented on the estimated epipolar geometry to compute the rotation and translations between a camera pair. A calibration method for stereo distributed camera networks called Lighthouse is proposed in [Jannotti and Mao, 2006], in which 3D point sets and geographic hash tables (GHTs) are used to localize and orient camera nodes. This method matches "point packs" constructed from 3D points, categorizing them according to a geometric hash function via the GHT, and then merges the nodes into ever-larger groups by propagating point packs to other groups. Virtual calibration object created by two LED markers is used in [Kurillo et al., 2008] for wide-area calibration. Calibration is performed by waiving the calibration bar over the camera coverage area. The initial pose of the cameras is calculated using essential matrix decompositions. Global calibration is solved by automatically constructing a weighted vision graph and finding optimal transformation paths between the cameras.

To deal with inconsistent parameter estimates in distributed camera networks, a belief propagation based distributed camera network calibration approach is proposed in [Devarajan et al., 2008b, Devarajan and Radke, 2007]. The state at a camera contains the pose (expressed in spherical angles and distances) and the calibration parameters (such as focal length) for itself and its neighbors in the vision graph. The initial measurement corresponding to the state is locally obtained by selecting a set of feature points visible to the camera and its neighbors and then performing self-calibration on this set of points. Through the belief propagation algorithm, the messages about common camera parameters are passed along the edges of the vision graph, so that the inconsistent estimates of camera parameters are iteratively brought closer together.

By assuming that one camera in a network is calibrated, a spanning tree based distributed calibration algorithm is presented in [Elhamifar and Vidal, 2009]. It is shown that Kruppa's equations for a pair of cameras (one calibrated and the other not) become linear. Therefore, given the point correspondence between these two cameras, in addition to their relative pose (translation and rotation), some of the unknown calibration parameters can be estimated. For a camera network, starting from the calibrated camera and using its correspondence with neighboring cameras, all its neighbors can be localized and calibrated. Through this process, the calibration and localization information is propagated along a spanning tree of the network, until the entire network is calibrated and localized. Then if a object is observed by this camera network, its 3D pose can be estimated using a consensus based method as describe below.

3.4.3 DISTRIBUTED POSE ESTIMATION

Consider a calibrated and localized camera network, i.e., each camera knows its calibration matrix K_i and its pose $h_i = (U_i, Z_i) \in SE(3) = \{(R, T) : R \in SO(3), T \in \mathbb{R}^3\}$, with respect to the world reference frame. Suppose that an object is visible to all the N cameras in the network. It is also assumed that a geometric model of the 3-D object is available and each camera can individually estimate the pose of the object $g_i = (\tilde{R}_i, \tilde{T}_i) \in SE(3)$ with respect to its own reference frame. Thus, the pose of the object with respect to the world reference frame can be easily calculated as

$$(R_i, T_i) = (U_i \tilde{R}_i, U_i \tilde{T}_i + Z_i) .$$

However, due to noise, such estimates are not geometrically consistent among cameras, i.e., they are not same with respect to the world reference frame. Therefore, the goal is achieve an average estimate of the pose in a distributed manner by only exchanging information between neighboring cameras.

Consensus on SE(3)

The classic consensus algorithms are designed to operate on Euclidean measurements, while the main challenge is that the space for pose is a nonlinear Riemannian manifold. Therefore, average consensus algorithms need to be extended to the non-Euclidean case of $SE(3)$. The work of [Tron et al., 2008] shows how to extend the standard consensus algorithms onto the space of the pose, $SE(3)$, as we briefly review below.

Since any pose can be represented with a rotation and a translation, $SE(3)$ is equivalent to $SO(3) \times \mathbb{R}^3$. If we know the average rotation, the average translation can be obtained through standard consensus process. Then the focus of pose consensus estimation is on developing consensus algorithms for rotation space, $SO(3)$. Denoting the geodesic distance in $SO(3)$ as $d_{SO(3)}(R_i, R_j)$, $R_i, R_j \in SO(3)$, the Fréchet mean $\bar{R}$ can be defined as

$$\bar{R} = \arg \min_{R \in SO(3)} \sum_i d_{SO(3)}(R, R_i). \tag{3.22}$$

In [Tron et al., 2008], the Fréchet mean is estimated using a Riemannian gradient descent scheme, i.e., for the estimation of $\bar{R}$ of camera C_k at the $(l + 1)^{th}$ iteration, $\bar{R}_k^{(l+1)}$ is updated along the geodesic corresponding to the covariant derivative direction as

$$\bar{R}_k^{(l+1)} = \bar{R}_k^{(l)} \exp \left(\varepsilon \sum_{i=1}^{N} a_{ik} \log((\bar{R}_k^{(l)})^T \bar{R}_i^{(l)}) \right), \tag{3.23}$$

where a_{ik} represents the (i, k) element of the adjacency matrix of the camera network topology.

In [Tron et al., 2008], the algorithm was tested on a simulated network with 20 cameras connected with a k-regular graph with $k = 6$. It was shown that compared to the initial rotation error, which was on the order of 10, the rotation error for the consensus estimate was on the order of 10^{-2}.

3.5   CONCLUSIONS

This chapter motivated the need for distributed vision algorithms and described its relationship to the area of multi-agent systems. Although each agent, equipped with cameras, is an independent entity, it needs to cooperate with other agents and arrive at a coordinated decision. The well-known consensus framework was explained in detail and its applications in tracking, data association and calibration described. Future research in this area holds tremendous potential in providing deeper mathematical insights into distributed video analysis algorithms, as well as opening up novel application scenarios.

CHAPTER 4

Object and Activity Recognition

In the previous chapters, we have looked into the problem of tracking in a camera network. Recognition is the other major challenge in computer vision applications and is the focus of this chapter. Since both object and activity recognition are well-studied problems, we focus on the specific issues that are characteristic of recognition in a network of cameras.

Recognition algorithms rely on the ability to extract reliable features and this can be a computationally expensive process. This calls for the development of schemes that can be implemented efficiently in low power environments and with limited communication resources between the cameras. We describe a recently proposed scheme that exploits compressive sensing theory to develop an object recognition approach for power and bandwidth constrained video sensor networks.

The domain of activity recognition has many challenging problems that are currently being addressed by a large group of researchers [Nayak et al., 2011, Turaga et al., 2008]. These include developing appropriate descriptors, classification mechanisms and the incorporation of contextual information, either from humans or other automated processing modules. In the domain of camera networks which usually cover a large field-of-view, the ability to correlate similar activity patterns across different temporal and spatial scales is of high importance. We describe an approach that addresses this issue later in this chapter. Representing activities evolving over wide areas and long time horizons requires developing mechanisms for representing atomic events and their spatio-temporal evolution. A method based on using topic models is described here.

In Chapter 3, we introduced consensus-based algorithms for distributed video analysis and showed how they can be adapted for tracking and pose estimation problems. In this chapter, we present a distributed activity recognition scheme whereby individual decisions at the camera nodes are fused together in a consensus framework.

4.1 OBJECT RECOGNITION

Object recognition is one of the most fundamental tasks in computer vision. Single-view object recognition is often challenged by factors like viewing angle, environmental conditions, occlusion and clutter. Extending the domain to multiple-views can cope with some of these challenges, but requires the ability to correlate between the views. Within the context of camera networks, we are interested in analyzing the issues particular to this application domain. As low-power network-enabled sensing devices have become popular in the recent years, distributed processing, which is naturally very appropriate for such networked sensors, is an additional issue that needs to be addressed.

For multi-view object recognition to work, correspondence between different views is necessary. When multiple images from different views share a set of common visual features, this correspondence can be established. SIFT (Scale-Invariant Feature Transform) [Lowe, 1999] features have been very popular for solving the multi-view object feature correspondence problem. In recent works, such as [Ferrari et al., 2004, Thomas et al., 2006], the prior spatial distribution of specific features was utilized to guide the multi-view matching process and improve the recognition. In [Yeo et al., 2008], the concept of random projection was used to estimate reliable feature correspondence between cameras communicating under rate constraints. In [Christoudias et al., 2008], a multi-view SIFT feature selection algorithm was proposed where it was shown that the number of SIFT features that need to be transmitted to the central server could be reduced by considering the joint distribution of the features among multiple camera views of a common object. Recently, a framework that performs distributed object recognition in band-limited smart camera networks was presented in [Yang et al., 2009]. Below, we briefly review this framework.

4.1.1   OBJECT RECOGNITION UNDER RESOURCE CONSTRAINTS

In [Yang et al., 2009], a camera network with star topology was assumed where each sensor was a low-power device and connected to the base-station with a bandwidth limited single-hop interface. The sensors would process their own observation to extract visual features, compress them and send to the base station for decompression and fusion. It was assumed that the cameras did not communicate with each other. The proposed multi-view compression framework extracted and compressed SIFT-based object histogram features. To design such a framework, three important properties of multiple-view image histogram were considered, namely, histogram sparsity, histogram non-negativity and multiple-view joint sparsity. On the base station side, multiple decoding schemes based on distributed compressive sensing theory were studied to simultaneously recover the multiple-view object features. Finally, a combined decision was made on the object class. We provide some details below.

First, at each node, using SIFT feature detector, viewpoint-invariant features were extracted from the corresponding images. Each of these local features were called codewords. The codewords from multiple object classes and training examples were clustered based on their visual similarities into a vocabulary or codebook. Here, hierarchical k-means was used to perform this clustering. Given such a large codebook over different object classes, an example image can be described using a histogram of the codewords which is called the SIFT histogram. If the number of object classes are large, the SIFT histogram would be *sparse*. Due to this sparsity, for a particular image, most of the values in this histogram were zero or close to zero. The SIFT histogram $\mathbf{x}$ at a particular node i was decomposed as

$$\mathbf{x}_i = \tilde{\mathbf{x}} + \mathbf{z}_i, \tag{4.1}$$

where $\tilde{\mathbf{x}}$ is the non-negative part of the feature that is common across different cameras, and $\mathbf{z}_i$ is the non-negative part that, in addition with the common part $\tilde{\mathbf{x}}$, makes up the original unique SIFT histogram $\mathbf{x}_i$ at each node.

Based on this representation, the authors formulate the object recognition problem as follows.

1. At each camera, construct an encoding function $f : \mathbf{x}_i \in \mathbb{R}^D \mapsto \mathbf{y}_i \in \mathbb{R}^d (d < D)$ that compresses the histogram.

2. On the base station, once $\mathbf{y}_1, \mathbf{y}_2, ..., \mathbf{y}_L$ are received, simultaneously recover the histogram signals $\mathbf{x}_1, \mathbf{x}_2, ..., \mathbf{x}_L$ and classify the object class.

The details of the encoding and decoding strategies can be found in [Yang et al., 2009].

Experimentations were performed on a real-time system called CITRIC as well as on the publicly available multi-camera object dataset COIL-100. In the real-time CITRIC system, it took about 10-20 s to extract SIFT features from the captured 320×240 grayscale images and to transmit the compressed histograms, $\mathbf{y}$, to the base station through a 250Kbps network interface for each camera. At the base station, upon receiving $\mathbf{y}$ from L cameras, the original sparse histograms $\mathbf{x}$ were computed. Support vector machine (SVM) was used at the base station to classify the object class and majority voting was used to get the final fused decision on the object's class.

The COIL-100 dataset consists of 72 views of 100 objects imaged from 0 to 360 degrees in 5 degree increments. When no compression was present, i.e., the complete histograms were sent (i.e. 991-D feature), about 95% accuracy was achieved which would be the upper-bound for the compressed schemes later used. With a compressed signal of 200 dimensions using random projection method, 80% accuracy was achieved, which remained about the same while using a compressed signal of 600 dimensions. Using information from multiple cameras, the fusion of 3 cameras approached the upper-bound of 95% accuracy using the 600 dimensional compressed signal.

The contribution of the paper lies in proposing a novel solution for distributed object recognition in band-limited smart camera networks. Future research in this direction should look into developing mechanisms to classify and associate multiple objects in the scene. The extension of the compressed sensing algorithms to dynamical processes, like recognition of activities, is another interesting area of future research.

4.2   TIME-DELAYED CORRELATION ANALYSIS

For low-quality surveillance videos with severe inter-object occlusion, it is difficult to obtain reliable tracks of objects, either intra-camera or inter-camera, for multi-camera activity analysis. In [Loy et al., 2010], an approach was proposed to model the time-delayed correlations among activities observed in multiple cameras. In this approach, each camera view was first decomposed automatically into regions based on the correlation of object dynamics across different spatial locations in all camera views. A Cross Canonical Correlation Analysis (xCCA) was then formulated to discover and quantify the time-delayed correlations of regional activities observed within and across multiple camera views. It was shown that learning the time-delayed activity correlations can be used for: (i) spatial and temporal topology inference of a camera network; (ii) robust person re-identification; and (iii) global activity interpretation and temporal segmentation of the video. We provide a brief overview of the approach below.

4.2.1   SCENE DECOMPOSITION AND ACTIVITY REPRESENTATION

Given a set of training video sequences, the scene viewed by M cameras is segmented into N regions, $\mathcal{R}$, according to the spatial-temporal distribution of activity patterns, i.e.,

$$\mathcal{R} = \{\mathcal{R}_n | n = 1, ..., N\}. \tag{4.2}$$

To account for intensity changes in real-world surveillance videos, a background model is formulated by adapting the background image to the intensity level of the current frame prior to background subtraction. To extract the activity pattern, the image frame of a camera view is first divided into equal-sized blocks with 10×10 pixels each. The foreground pixels are then detected through background subtraction. The foreground pixels are categorized as either static or moving via frame differencing. Then activity patterns of a block are represented as a bivariate time-series,

$$\begin{aligned}
\mathbf{u_b} &= (u_{\mathbf{b},1}, ..., u_{\mathbf{b},t}, ..., u_{\mathbf{b},T}), \\
\mathbf{v_b} &= (v_{\mathbf{b},1}, ..., v_{\mathbf{b},t}, ..., v_{\mathbf{b},T}),
\end{aligned} \tag{4.3}$$

where $\mathbf{b}$ is the two-dimensional coordinates of a block, T is the number of frames used for training, $u_{\mathbf{b},t}$ and $v_{\mathbf{b},t}$ are the percentage of static and moving foreground pixels, respectively, within the block at t^{th} frame.

After extracting features, the blocks are grouped into regions according to the similarity of their spatio-temporal activity patterns. Two blocks are considered similar and grouped together if they have high correlations in both static and moving activity patterns. A correlation distance is defined as

$$\bar{r} = 1 - |r|, \tag{4.4}$$

where r is the Pearson's correlation coefficient [Liao, 2005]. Then an affinity matrix $\mathbf{A} = \{A_{ij}\} \in \mathbb{R}^{B \times B}$ is constructed, where B is the total number of blocks in the camera view and A_{ij} is defined as

$$A_{ij} = \begin{cases} \exp\left(-\frac{(\bar{r}_{ij}^{\mathbf{u}})^2}{2\sigma_i^{\mathbf{u}}\sigma_j^{\mathbf{u}}}\right) \exp\left(-\frac{(\bar{r}_{ij}^{\mathbf{v}})^2}{2\sigma_i^{\mathbf{v}}\sigma_j^{\mathbf{v}}}\right) \exp\left(-\frac{\|\mathbf{b}_i - \mathbf{b}_j\|^2}{2\sigma_{\mathbf{b}}^2}\right), & \text{if } \|\mathbf{b}_i - \mathbf{b}_j\| \leq R \text{ and } i \neq j, \\ 0 & \text{otherwise}, \end{cases} \tag{4.5}$$

where $\bar{r}_{ij}^{\mathbf{u}}$ and $\bar{r}_{ij}^{\mathbf{v}}$ are the correlation distances of $\mathbf{u_b}$ and $\mathbf{v_b}$ between blocks i and j, and $[\sigma_i^{\mathbf{u}}, \sigma_j^{\mathbf{u}}]$ and $[\sigma_i^{\mathbf{v}}, \sigma_j^{\mathbf{v}}]$ are the correlation scaling factors for $\bar{r}_{ij}^{\mathbf{u}}$ and $\bar{r}_{ij}^{\mathbf{u}}$, respectively. The correlation scaling factors are defined as the mean correlation distance between the current block and all blocks within a radius R, with $\mathbf{b}_i$ and $\mathbf{b}_j$ being the coordinates of the two blocks. Similarly, the spatial scaling factor $\sigma_{\mathbf{b}}$ is defined as the mean spatial distance between the current block and all blocks within the radius R. $\mathbf{A}$ is then normalized by

$$\bar{\mathbf{A}} = \mathbf{L}^{-\frac{1}{2}} \mathbf{A} \mathbf{L}^{-\frac{1}{2}}, \tag{4.6}$$

where $\mathbf{L}$ is a diagonal matrix and $L_{ii} = \sum_{j=1}^{B} A_{ij}$. Next, the spectral clustering method proposed in [Zelnik-Manor and Perona, 2004] is employed to decompose each camera view into regions.

After the scene decomposition, regional activity patterns of a camera view are formed based on the local block activity patterns by

$$\hat{\mathbf{u}}_n = \frac{1}{|\mathcal{R}_n|} \sum_{\mathbf{b} \in \mathcal{R}_n} \mathbf{u_b},$$

$$\hat{\mathbf{v}}_n = \frac{1}{|\mathcal{R}_n|} \sum_{\mathbf{b} \in \mathcal{R}_n} \mathbf{v_b}, \tag{4.7}$$

where $|\mathcal{R}_n|$ is the number of blocks in region $\mathcal{R}_n$.

4.2.2   CROSS CANONICAL CORRELATION ANALYSIS

To measure the correlation of activities in a pair of regions in a camera network and to understand their temporal relationships, a Cross Canonical Correlation Analysis (xCCA) analysis was proposed in [Loy et al., 2010]. Canonical Correlation Analysis (CCA) [Hotelling, 1936] is used to measure how strongly two vector variables are correlated. As an extension of CCA, xCCA shifts one time series and computes its canonical correlations with the other. This is used to measure the correlation of two regional activities as a function of an unknown time lag, τ, applied to one of the two activity time series.

Let $\mathbf{x}_i(t)$ and $\mathbf{x}_j(t)$ denote the two regional activity time series observed in the ith and jth regions, respectively. For each time delay index τ, their canonical correlation is represented as $\rho_{\mathbf{x}_i,\mathbf{x}_j}(\tau)$ (see [Loy et al., 2010] for details of calculating ρ). The time delay that maximizes $\rho_{\mathbf{x}_i,\mathbf{x}_j}$ is computed as

$$\hat{\tau}_{\mathbf{x}_i,\mathbf{x}_j} = \arg\max_{\tau} \frac{\sum^{\Gamma} \rho_{\mathbf{x}_i,\mathbf{x}_j}(\tau)}{\Gamma}, \tag{4.8}$$

where $\Gamma = \min(rank(\mathbf{x}_i), rank(\mathbf{x}_j))$. The associated maximum canonical correlation is

$$\hat{\rho}_{\mathbf{x}_i,\mathbf{x}_j} = \frac{\sum^{\Gamma} \rho_{\mathbf{x}_i,\mathbf{x}_j}(\hat{\tau}_{\mathbf{x}_i,\mathbf{x}_j})}{\Gamma}. \tag{4.9}$$

4.2.3   APPLICATIONS

Topology Inference.   A camera topology is inferred from the regional activity correlation. Two cameras will be connected in the inferred topology if they contain connected regions which are defined as those with high correlation value and short time delay.

Person Re-identification.   Given the bounding boxes of two people, a and b, observed in different camera views, the associated inter-region correlation and time delay are determined. If the bounding box on a person overlaps N_r regions in the image space, the occupancy fractions of individual regions within the bounding box are denoted by

$$\mu = \{\mu_i | i = 1, ..., N_r\}, \quad \sum_{i=1}^{N_r} \mu_i = 1. \tag{4.10}$$

The correlation between regions occupied by a and b are calculated as

$$\hat{\rho}^{a,b} = \sum_{i=1}^{N_r^a} \mu_i^a \left(\sum_{j=1}^{N_r^b} \mu_j^b \hat{\rho}_{\mathbf{x}_i, \mathbf{x}_j} \right), \tag{4.11}$$

and the corresponding time delay is given as

$$\hat{\tau}^{a,b} = \sum_{i=1}^{N_r^a} \mu_i^a \left(\sum_{j=1}^{N_r^b} \mu_j^b \hat{\tau}_{\mathbf{x}_i, \mathbf{x}_j} \right). \tag{4.12}$$

Thus, the similarity score between a and b is computed as

$$S^{a,b} = \begin{cases} \bar{S}_{bha}^{a,b} \hat{\rho}^{a,b} & \text{if } 0 < t_{gap}^{a,b} < \alpha \hat{\tau}^{a,b}, \\ 0 & \text{otherwise,} \end{cases} \tag{4.13}$$

where $\bar{S}_{bha}^{a,b}$ is the Bhattacharyya distance between the color histograms of a and b, $t_{gap}^{a,b}$ is the time gap between observing a and b, and α is a factor that determines the maximum allowable transition time between cameras.

Global Activity Interpretation.   The reginal activities are grouped based on their correlation according to (4.9). The aligned regional activity patterns are used as inputs to train an Hidden Markov Model (HMM) to model the temporal dynamics of the global activity.

4.3   ACTIVITY ANALYSIS USING TOPIC MODELS

The problem of activity analysis in multiple camera views using topic models was addressed in [Wang et al., 2010a]. The cameras were static and synchronized but did not have to be calibrated. The proposed approach was built upon several basic concepts and assumptions as follows. There are paths in the physical world. Objects move along these paths and form different moving patterns, which are called *activities*. A path may be observed in multiple camera views and has spatial distributions in these views. A trajectory is a record of the positions of an object in a camera view. The points on trajectories are called observations. In this work, trajectories, which belong to the same activity but may be in different camera views, were grouped into one cluster and paths of objects across camera views were modeled probabilistically. The scene of a camera view was quantized into small cells and the probabilistic model was based on some assumptions of the spatial and temporal features related to activities: (i) cells located on the same path are likely to be connected by trajectories; (ii) trajectories passing through the same path belong to the same activity; and (iii) it is likely for trajectories of the same object observed in different camera views to be on the same path in the real world and belong to the same activity.

In the approach proposed by Wang et al. [2010a], trajectories that are in different camera views and have close temporal extents are first connected by edges. A probabilistic model representing the distribution of an activity in low-level feature spaces of different camera views can be learned. A trajectory is computed based on the observations of the activities. Two neighboring trajectories connected by an edge should have similar distributions over activities. Trajectories are clustered according to the major assigned activities among their observations. The distributions of activities over feature spaces in different camera views model the regions of paths across cameras.

4.3.1   PROBABILISTIC MODEL

This work is related to topic models used for word-document analysis. The topic models, such as Probabilistic Latent Semantic Analysis (pLSA) [Hofmann, 1999] and Latent Dirichlet Allocation (LDA) [Blei et al., 2003], assume that a document is a mixture of topics, and cluster words that often co-occur in the same documents into one topic. In this work, documents are trajectories, words are observations, and topics are activities.

Assume that there are totally M trajectories and each trajectory j has N_j observations. Each observation i on trajectory j can be represented by a visual word value w_{ji} which is an index of a global codebook. Observations are clustered to one of the K activity categories and z_{ji} is used to denote the activity label of observation i on trajectory j. Each activity, k, has a multinomial distribution, ϕ_k, over the global codebook. Each trajectory, j, has a multinomial distribution over K activities and its distribution parameter is a random variable which is denoted as θ_j. Activity labels, $\{z_{ji}\}$, of the observations are sampled from θ_j. By adopting the probabilistic model in LDA, the joint distribution of $\{\phi_k\}$, $\{\theta_j\}$, $\{z_{ji}\}$ and $\{w_{ji}\}$ can be modeled as

$$
\begin{aligned}
&p(\{\phi_k\}, \{\theta_j\}, \{z_{ji}\}, \{w_{ji}\} | \alpha, \beta, \gamma) \\
&= \prod_{j=1}^{M} \left[\frac{\prod_{k=1}^{K} \Gamma(\alpha + \gamma \sum_{j' \in \Omega_j} n_{j'k})}{\Gamma(K \cdot \alpha + \gamma \sum_{j' \in \Omega_j} \sum_{k=1}^{K} n_{j'k})} \mathrm{Dir}(\theta_j; \alpha + \gamma \sum_{j' \in \Omega_j} n_{j'1}, ..., \alpha + \gamma \sum_{j' \in \Omega_j} n_{j'K}) \right] \\
&\quad \prod_{k=1}^{K} \mathrm{Dir}(\phi_k; \beta) \prod_{j=1}^{M} \prod_{i=1}^{N_j} (\theta_{j z_{ji}} \cdot \phi_{z_{ji} w_{ji}}),
\end{aligned}
\tag{4.14}
$$

where $\Gamma(\cdot)$ is the Gamma function, n_{jk} is the number of observations assigned to activity k on trajectory j, and Ω_j is the set of trajectories connected with j. $\mathrm{Dir}(\cdot; \cdot)$ is Dirichlet distribution with flat hyperparameter β. γ is a positive scale - a larger γ puts a stronger smoothness constraint, while if $\gamma = 0$ then the trajectories are treated to be independent. The interested reader should refer to [Wang et al., 2010a] for more mathematical details.

The goal is to estimate activity labels $\{z_{ji}\}$ and activity models $\{\phi_k\}$. The inference is done by Gibbs sampling, as follows:

$$
\begin{aligned}
&p(\{z_{ji}\}, \{w_{ji}\}|\alpha, \beta, \gamma) \\
&= \int_{\{\phi_k\}} \int_{\{\theta_j\}} p(\{\phi_k\}, \{\theta_j\}, \{z_{ji}\}, \{w_{ji}\}|\alpha, \beta, \gamma) d\{\theta_j\} d\{\phi_k\} \\
&\propto \prod_k \frac{\prod_w \Gamma(\beta + m_{kw})}{\Gamma(W \cdot \beta + m_k)} \prod_j \frac{\prod_k \Gamma(\alpha + n_{jk} + \gamma \sum_{j' \in \Omega_j} n_{j'k})}{\Gamma(K \cdot \alpha + n_j + \gamma \sum_{j' \in \Omega_j} n_{j'})},
\end{aligned}
\tag{4.15}
$$

where W is the size of the global codebook, m_{kw} is the number of observations with value w that are assigned to activity k, m_k is the total number of observations assigned to activity k, n_{jk} is the number of observations on trajectory j that are assigned to activity k, and n_j is the total number of observations on trajectory j. The conditional distribution of z_{ji} given all the other activity labels $\mathbf{z}^{-ji}$ is

$$
p(z_{ji} = k|\mathbf{z}^{-ji}, \{w_{ji}\}, \alpha, \beta, \gamma) \propto \frac{\beta + m_{kw}^{-ji}}{W \cdot \beta + m_k^{-ji}} \frac{\alpha + n_{jk}^{-ji} + \gamma \sum_{j' \in \Omega_j} n_{j'k}}{K \cdot \alpha + n_j^{-ji} + \gamma \sum_{j' \in \Omega_j} n_{j'}},
\tag{4.16}
$$

where m_{kw}^{-ji}, m_k^{-ji}, n_{jk}^{-ji} and n_j^{-ji} are similar to m_{kw}, m_k, n_{jk} and n_j except that they exclude observation i on trajectory j. γ controls the weight of neighboring trajectories. The model of activities can be estimated from any single sample of $\{z_{ji}\}$ as

$$
\hat{\phi}_{kw} = \frac{\beta + m_{kw}}{W \cdot \beta + m_k}.
\tag{4.17}
$$

4.3.2 LABELING TRAJECTORIES INTO ACTIVITIES

A trajectory is labeled as activity k if most of its observation are assigned to activity k. After learning and fixing the activity model at the end of Gibbs sampling using (4.16) and (4.17), a observation is labeled as

$$
z_{ji} = \arg \max_k \hat{\phi}_{kw_{ji}}.
\tag{4.18}
$$

4.4 DISTRIBUTED ACTIVITY RECOGNITION

There are many methods on multi-view activity recognition, (e.g., [Wang et al., 2007, Weinland et al., 2007]), but the information of multiple views is fused centrally. In this section, we consider the problem of activity recognition in a camera network where processing power is distributed across the network and there is no central processor accumulating and analyzing all the data. Each camera computes a similarity measure of the observed activities in its views against a dictionary of pre-defined activities.

Also, the transition probability between activities is known. This is a common assumption used in many activity recognition approaches and can be learned *a priori* from training data [Cham and Rehg, 1999, Doucet et al., 2001, Liao et al., 2005, North et al., 2000, Rittscher and Black, 1999]. If no such information is available, the transition matrix can be assumed to be uniform. Based on the computed similarities at each camera node and the learned transition matrices, we show how to compute the consensus estimate in a probabilistic framework. Essentially, the consensus is a probability of similarity of the observed activity against the dictionary taking into account the decisions of the individual cameras. More details of this work can be found in [Song et al., 2010b].

4.4.1   CONSENSUS FOR ACTIVITY RECOGNITION

Let us assume that there are N_c cameras viewing a person performing some actions. The observation of camera C_i in the kth time interval is denoted as $O_i(k)$, $i = 1, \ldots, N_c$. Let $\mathbf{O}(k)$ be the collection of observations from all the cameras, i.e., $\mathbf{O}(k) = \{O_1(k), \ldots, O_{N_c}(k)\}$. Its history is $\mathcal{O}^k = \{\mathbf{O}(1), \ldots, \mathbf{O}(k)\}$. The problem of activity recognition can be formulated so as to estimate the conditional probability, $P(y(k)|\mathcal{O}^k)$, where $y(k) \in \{1, \ldots, Y\}$ is the label of the class of activity in a dictionary of Y activities with history $\mathcal{Y}^k = \{y(1), \ldots, y(k)\}$.

The state transitions of activity class y are assumed to be governed by the transition matrix for a 1st order Markov chain [Rittscher and Black, 1999], i.e.,

$$P(y(k) = a|y(k-1) = a', \mathcal{Y}^{k-2}) = P(y(k) = a|y(k-1) = a') = m(a', a). \tag{4.19}$$

$m(a', a)$ can be learned *a priori* from training data; if no such information is available, the transition matrix can be assumed to be uniform. Given $y(k)$, observation $\mathbf{O}(k)$ is assumed to be independent of other observations and states, i.e.,

$$P(\mathbf{O}(k)|\mathcal{Y}^k, \mathcal{O}^{k-1}) = P(\mathbf{O}(k)|y(k)). \tag{4.20}$$

Based on Bayes' rule and above Markov chain assumption, it was shown that the following relationship holds.

Result 4.1

$$
\begin{aligned}
P(y(k)|\mathcal{O}^k) \;=\; & \frac{1}{P(\mathbf{O}(k)|\mathcal{O}^{k-1})} \\
& \cdot \prod_{j=1}^{N_c} P(O_j(k)|y(k)) \left(\sum_{y(k-1)} P(y(k)|y(k-1))P(y(k-1)|\mathcal{O}^{k-1}) \right),
\end{aligned} \tag{4.21}
$$

where $\sum_{y(k)}$ mean summing over all values of $y(k) = 1, \ldots, Y$.   □

Analysis of Result 4.1: By observing the right-hand side of equation (4.21), we notice that $P(O_j(k)|y(k))$, $j = 1, \ldots, N_c$ is the likelihood of camera C_j's observation. The first term of the right-hand side is a constant with respect to $y(k)$, so that it can be treated as a normalization factor and denoted by $\gamma(k)$, i.e.,

$$\gamma(k) \triangleq \frac{1}{P(\mathbf{O}(k)|\mathcal{O}^{k-1})}.$$

So (4.21) can be rewritten as

$$P(y(k)|\mathcal{O}^k) = \gamma(k) \prod_{j=1}^{N_c} P(O_j(k)|y(k)) \left(\sum_{y(k-1)} P(y(k)|y(k-1))P(y(k-1)|\mathcal{O}^{k-1}) \right). \quad (4.22)$$

The state of the activity at camera C_i is defined as $\mathbf{w}_i = \left[w_i^1, w_i^2, \cdots, w_i^Y \right]^T$, where

$$w_i^a \triangleq P(y(k) = a|\mathcal{O}^k), a = 1, \ldots, Y.$$

The likelihood of camera C_i's observation is denoted by $\mathbf{v}_i = \left[v_i^1, v_i^2, \cdots, v_i^Y \right]^T$, where

$$v_i^a \triangleq P(O_i(k)|y(k) = a), a = 1, \ldots, Y.$$

Thus,

$$\begin{aligned} w_i^a(k) &= \gamma(k) \prod_{j=1}^{N_c} P(O_j(k)|y(k) = a) \\ &\quad \cdot \left(\sum_{y(k-1)} P(y(k) = a|y(k-1) = a')P(y(k-1) = a'|\mathcal{O}^{k-1}) \right) \\ &= \gamma(k) \prod_{j=1}^{N_c} v_j^a(k) \left(\sum_{a'=1}^{Y} m(a', a)w_i^{a'}(k-1) \right) \end{aligned} \quad (4.23)$$

Regarding the normalization factor $\gamma(k)$, the following result holds.

Result 4.2

$$\gamma(k) = \left(\sum_{y(k)} \prod_{j=1}^{N_c} P(O_j(k)|y(k)) \cdot \left(\sum_{y(k-1)} P(y(k)|y(k-1))P(y(k-1)|\mathcal{O}^{k-1}) \right) \right)^{-1}.$$

$\square$

Result 4.3   The local activity recognition procedure for node i based on fusion of the recognition results in all the cameras is

$$v_i^a(k) = P(O_i(k)|y(k) = a), a = 1, \ldots, Y,$$

$$w_i^a(k) = \gamma(k) \prod_{j=1}^{N_c} v_j^a(k) \left(\sum_{a'=1}^{Y} m(a', a) w_i^{a'}(k-1) \right), a = 1, \ldots, Y, \quad (4.24)$$

$$\gamma(k) = \left(\sum_{a=1}^{Y} \prod_{j=1}^{N_c} v_j^a(k) \left(\sum_{a'=1}^{Y} m(a', a) w_i^{a'}(k-1) \right) \right)^{-1}.$$

□

The proof of Result 4.3 follows directly from Results 4.1 and 4.2. Details can be found in [Song et al., 2010b].

Since each camera can only communicate with its neighbors, there is no guarantee that the estimates of this local activity recognition algorithm remain cohesive among nodes. The authors use an ad hoc approach by implementing a consensus step right after the estimation step to reduce the disagreement regarding the estimates obtained in Result 4.3, leading to Algorithm 4. This consensus approach is similar to the one proposed in [Olfati-Saber, 2007] for the Kalman-Consensus filtering.

The cameras that exchange information in the consensus stage are defined based on the communication constraints; therefore, it is possible that a camera involved in the consensus does not view the activity. In this case, such a camera transmits a value of $\mathbf{v}_i = \frac{1}{Y}\mathbf{1}_Y$, i.e., by assuming equal likelihood for all possible action classes.

An Example of Distributed Activity Recognition

In [Song et al., 2010b], the authors showed detailed experimental results to validate the consensus approach for distributed activity recognition. Here we summarize the main result to illustrate the strength of a consensus algorithm. In Figure 4.1, we show results to compare the probability of correct match for individual cameras versus their consensus on the IXMAS dataset [Weinland et al., 2007]. In the dataset, there are sequences of images of different people doing several actions. The actions considered were: looking at watch, scratching head, sit, wave hand, punch, kick and pointing a gun. Every possible subset of the five cameras were used by considering five, four, three and two cameras to determine their consensus and show that the consensus result is better than an individual camera, on average. This result shows the advantage of the consensus process.

In Figure 4.2, we show the similarity matrices, i.e., the probability of match for each test activity (the row of a matrix). The more white the cell block is, the test data it refers to is detected with more probability as that action. Five of the images represent the similarity matrix for the test data captured by each camera and the sixth image shows the similarity matrix of the consensus for all of these cameras. The similarity scores of correct matching are the diagonal values of the similarity matrix. Comparing with other values in the matrix, the higher the diagonal values (brighter in the image) are, the less confusing the recognition result is. By comparing the similarity matrix of

---

Algorithm 4 Distributed consensus based activity recognition algorithm performed by every C_i at step k.

Input: $\bar{\mathbf{w}}_i(k-1)$

for each person that is being viewed by C_i and the set of its neighbors $\{\mathcal{C}_i^c\}$ **do**

    Obtain observations $O_i(k)$

    Compute local likelihood

$$
\mathbf{v}_i(k) = \begin{bmatrix} v_i^1(k) \\ \vdots \\ v_i^Y(k) \end{bmatrix} = \begin{bmatrix} P(O_i(k)|y(k)=1) \\ \vdots \\ P(O_i(k)|y(k)=Y) \end{bmatrix}
$$

    Send $\mathbf{v}_i(k)$ to neighboring cameras $\mathcal{C}_i^n$

    Receive $\mathbf{v}_j(k)$ from all cameras $C_j \in \mathcal{C}_i^n$

    Fuse information to estimate activity state

$$
\mathbf{w}_i(k) = \begin{bmatrix} w_i^1(k) \\ \vdots \\ w_i^Y(k) \end{bmatrix} = \begin{bmatrix} \gamma(k) \prod_{j\in(C_i\cup\mathcal{C}_i^n)} v_j^1(k) \left(\sum_{a'=1}^{Y} m(a',1)\bar{w}_i^{a'}(k-1) \right) \\ \vdots \\ \gamma(k) \prod_{j\in(C_i\cup\mathcal{C}_i^n)} v_j^Y(k) \left(\sum_{a'=1}^{Y} m(a',Y)\bar{w}_i^{a'}(k-1) \right) \end{bmatrix}
$$

$$
= \gamma(k) \prod_{j\in(C_i\cup\mathcal{C}_i^n)} \Lambda(\mathbf{v}_j(k))\mathbf{M}^T \bar{\mathbf{w}}_i(k-1),
$$

$$
\gamma(k) = \left(\sum_{a=1}^{Y} \prod_{j\in(C_i\cup\mathcal{C}_i^n)} v_j^a(k) \left(\sum_{a'=1}^{Y} m(a',a)\bar{w}_i^{a'}(k-1) \right) \right)^{-1}
$$

$$
= \left(\mathbf{1}_Y^T \cdot \prod_{j\in(C_i\cup\mathcal{C}_i^n)} \Lambda(\mathbf{v}_j(k))\mathbf{M}^T \bar{\mathbf{w}}_i(k-1) \right)^{-1}, \tag{4.25}
$$

where $\mathbf{M}$ is a $Y \times Y$ matrix with $(i,j)^{th}$ element to be $m(i,j)$,

$$
\Lambda(\mathbf{v}_j(k)) = \begin{bmatrix} v_j^1(k) & & \\ & \ddots & \\ & & v_j^Y(k) \end{bmatrix}, \text{ and } \mathbf{1}_Y = \begin{bmatrix} 1 \\ \vdots \\ 1 \end{bmatrix} \text{ with } Y \text{ elements.}
$$

  repeat

    Send $\mathbf{w}_i(k)$ to neighboring cameras $\mathcal{C}_i^n$

    Receive $\mathbf{w}_j(k)$ from all cameras $C_j \in \mathcal{C}_i^n$

    Compute the Consensus state estimate

$$
\bar{\mathbf{w}}_i(k) = \mathbf{w}_i(k) + \epsilon \sum_{j\in\mathcal{C}_i^n} (\mathbf{w}_j(k) - \mathbf{w}_i(k))
$$

  until either a predefined iteration number is reached or $\sum_{j\in\mathcal{C}_i^n}(\mathbf{w}_j(k) - \mathbf{w}_i(k))$ is smaller than a predefined small value

end for

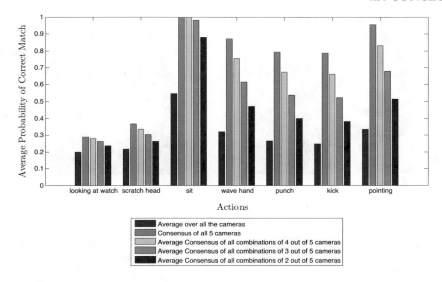

Figure 4.1: Comparison of average probability of correct match for individual camera and their consensus for all the activities. Their are seven sets of bars for seven different actions and in each set, there are five bars where the leftmost one (blue) is the average probability of correct match for individual cameras and the next four bars the average probability of correct match of the consensus over all the combinations of cameras taking, respectively, five, four, three and two out of five cameras. (From [Song et al., 2010b])

consensus with the test data captured by each camera (compare (f) with (a)-(e)), it is clear that the recognition result after consensus has less confusion than others.

In [Song et al., 2010b], it was also shown how this algorithm can be applied to sequences containing multiple activities. For example, recognition results on a sequence of punch-kick-punch-kick were given.

4.5 CONCLUSIONS

Camera networks pose a number of unique challenges to recognition algorithms. Multiple views need to be fused and activities evolving over wide areas and long time horizons need to be considered. Communication and computational resources can be limited and the recognition algorithms need to be aware of these constraints. Although there have been a few methods that have looked at the issue of recognition in camera networks, the above-mentioned challenges very much remain at the forefront of research in this area. Recognition algorithms that are aware of the network-level constraints are an especially interesting area of research with only a few existing results.

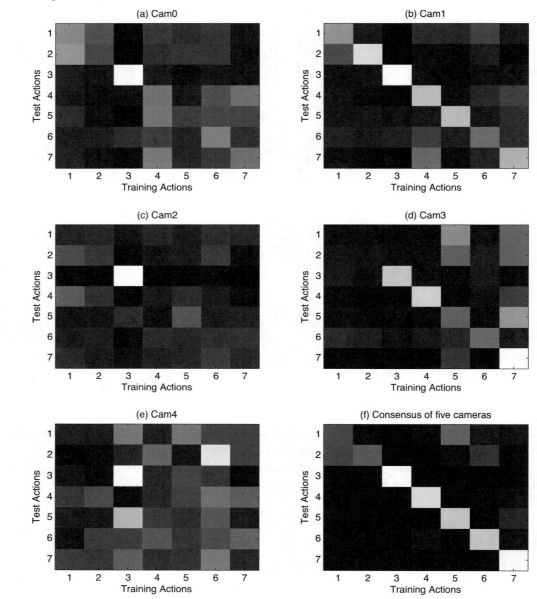

Figure 4.2: (a-e) Similarity matrices of the activities for the cameras Cam0, Cam1, Cam2, Cam3 and Cam4; (f) Similarity matrix of the activities for the consensus of all these cameras. Actions 1–7 are looking at watch, scratching head, sit, wave hand, punch, kick and pointing a gun, respectively, all from the IXMAS dataset. (From [Song et al., 2010b])

CHAPTER 5

Active Sensing

Networks of cameras are rich information sources for many tasks related to security and surveillance, environmental monitoring, disaster response, etc. In such applications, it is often necessary that the cameras coordinate between themselves to sense, learn and reason about the environment, leading to a multi-agent network of cameras. The agents are given some high-level objectives and rules to perform certain tasks. As an example, the network might be tasked with tracking all moving objects, obtaining identity information for each, and understanding their behaviors. The rules entail certain video analysis tasks that need to be performed; for example, tracking involves obtaining the positions of the targets in the 3D world, person recognition may be obtained from frontal facial shots, understanding behaviors may require obtaining high-resolution shots of the entire person or groups of people when they are in close proximity. The entire process may require that the camera network adjust its sensing parameters based on analysis of the previously acquired images, thus leading to an integrated sensing and analysis framework. It requires collaboration between the cameras on both the sensing and analysis aspects and allows for specific images to be obtained at times of opportunity.

Integrated sensing and analysis is referred to as active sensing [Blake and Yuille, 1992, J. Aloimonos, 1988]. Here, we focus on active sensing in a distributed camera network and term it as *collaborative sensing*. The goal of collaborative sensing is to develop a distributed strategy for coordinated camera control that relies on local decision-making at the camera nodes, while being aligned with the suitable global criteria for scene analysis which are specified by the user. The cameras coordinate between themselves to satisfy the different objectives, autonomously deciding not only *how* to perform the tasks, but also *when* to perform each of the tasks. In this chapter, we review a variety of methods that have been proposed in the area of active sensing in camera networks. Thereafter, we show how the problem of collaborative sensing can be solved by modeling the problem as a multi-player cooperative game in which the cameras are the players and are interested in optimizing their own utility. The game-theoretic framework is motivated by similar approaches in the multi-agent systems literature, but require significant modifications to be applicable to camera networks.

5.1 PROBLEM FORMULATION

The problem of collaborative sensing in a camera network envisions a number of cameras N_C placed in and around the region R under surveillance and a time-varying number of targets $N_T(t)$. These cameras have known fixed locations with dynamic pan ρ, tilt τ, and zoom ζ parameters. Each target T_j, for $j \in \{1, ..., N_T\}$, may have different criteria that must be satisfied by the camera network, e.g., the user may want to identify T_1 using facial recognition and determine what activity T_2 is doing using activity recognition. In another scenario, the user may be interested in observing the scene of a disaster zone to discover and monitor the state of people. Here, it may be important to place priority on those who are wounded or in need of aid. This scenario would require targets in R to have varying values of importance and varying requirements over time.

We assume that resources are available to perform all tasks (tracking, imaging, etc.) for all targets over the time that the system is used to monitor the region. However, resources may not available to perform all tasks for all targets at a given instant of time. For example, if there are fewer cameras than targets, we may not be able to simultaneously acquire high-resolution facial images for all targets. Hence, it becomes imperative to prioritize tasks based on scene analysis. The design of utility functions that model these network objectives and their solution in a decentralized camera network is discussed in this chapter.

5.1.1 ACTIVE SENSING OF DYNAMICAL PROCESSES

We assume that each of the cameras in the network has its own embedded target detection module, a distributed state-estimator that provides an estimate on the state of each target in the scene, and finally a distributed camera parameter (pan, tilt, zoom (PTZ)) selection mechanism. Consider the time interval $t \in (t_k, t_{k+1})$ where t_k is the time of the last set of images and t_{k+1} is the time scheduled for the next set of images. During this time interval, several processes must be accomplished (see Figure 5.1). Targets will be tracked using measurements from multiple cameras that may not have direct communication with each other. Other aspects, like the pose of the target or its activity label, may be estimated. Neighboring cameras will communicate with each other to come to a consensus about these parameters, as explained in Chapter 3.

Also, in this interval, each camera will select its dynamic PTZ parameters, (ρ, τ, ζ), to optimize a local value function. This local function is designed such that the solution is aligned with the global value function. Each image may contain multiple targets and each target may be imaged by multiple cameras. At the time that each camera selects its parameters for the image scheduled to occur at the future time t_{k+1}, the target locations at t_{k+1} are unknown. Based on the last set of imagery from time t_k, the target state estimation process provides a prior mean $\hat{\mathbf{x}}^j(k+1)^-$ and covariance matrix $\mathbf{P}^j(k+1)^-$ for all targets (i.e., $j = 1, \ldots, N_T$). Due to uncertainty in the target state $\mathbf{x}^j(k+1)$, there is a tradeoff in the camera parameter selection between tracking gain, imaging, and coverage risk.

Figure 5.2 depicts the series of temporal events. The first process is target detection. The target detection module in each camera takes its raw image and returns the image plane positions of each target recognized in the image. Communication between cameras is allowed to enhance the processes of feature detection and association for target recognition [Song and Roy-Chowdhury, 2007]. In Figure 5.2, the time of completion of this process is denoted as t_β. At t_β, each camera has computed the pixel coordinate measurement of each recognized target within its FOV. Assuming that target j is within the FOV of camera i, this image frame measurement of the pixel location

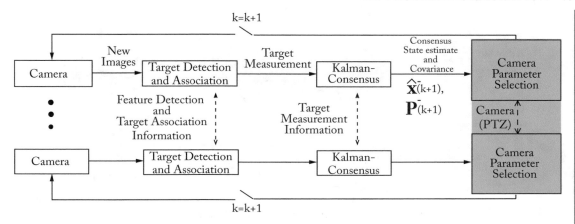

Figure 5.1: Overall system diagram depicting a framework for integrated sensing and analysis in a reconfigurable, distributed camera network. Information exchange shown is only between neighboring cameras. (Adapted from [Morye et al., 2011])

of target T_j by camera C_i, valid at time t_k, is denoted by $^i\mathbf{u}^j(k)$. This measurement is broadcast to neighboring cameras.

The second process is target state estimation. Using its own image plane position measurements and those received from the camera network, each camera implements a consensus state estimation algorithm [Morye et al., 2011, Olfati-Saber and Sandell, 2008], to compute a posterior mean $\hat{\mathbf{x}}^j(k)^+$ and covariance matrix $\mathbf{P}^j(k)^+$ for all targets (i.e., $j = 1, \ldots, N_T$). Using the posterior information from t_k and the assumed target model, the prior mean $\hat{\mathbf{x}}^j(k+1)^-$ and covariance matrix $\mathbf{P}^j(k+1)^-$ for all targets is computed as an input to the camera parameter selection process. This was explained in Section 3.3. In Figure 5.2, the time of availability of the prior information is indicated as t_δ.

The third process is collaborative selection of the camera parameters for the next image based on scene analysis. In addition to target state estimation, we are interested in obtaining high-resolution imagery for certain targets at opportune times. The importance of imagery for specific targets is indicated by weights $\{v_j\}_{j=1}^{N_T}$ in a utility function described later. This weight can be made to change subject to scene analysis or if prior high-resolution imagery of the target has been performed. Imagery from specific aspect angles may also be desirable and would be achieved using the assumption that the aspect angle is related to the direction of target motion. By including resolution specifications, aspect or viewing angle, and target importance in the utility function, we further enhance the performance of the network, by making opportunistic high-resolution imagery of targets possible.

In Figure 5.2, the parameter selection process occurs for $t \in (t_\delta, t_\epsilon)$, leaving the interval $t \in (t_\epsilon, t_{k+1})$ for the cameras to achieve the commanded parameter settings. The camera parameter

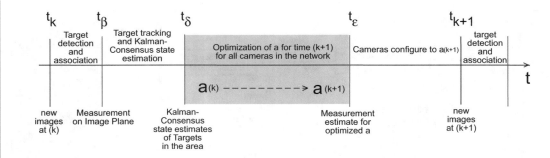

Figure 5.2: Timeline of events between image sample times. (From [Morye et al., 2011])

selection process is designed as a distributed optimization. Let $\mathbf{a}_i$, $\mathbf{a}_{-i}$, and $\mathbf{a}$, respectively, represent the vector of parameter settings for the i-th camera, all cameras other than the i-th camera, and all cameras. At the time that camera i is adjusting $\mathbf{a}_i$ the parameters in $\mathbf{a}_{-i}$ are held constant. Over the time interval $t \in (t_\delta, t_\epsilon)$, each camera will have various opportunities to adjust its parameter settings and communicate its revised settings to the network, such that the entire vector $\mathbf{a}$ converges towards the optimal settings for the upcoming images at t_{k+1}.

It must be noted that cameras take images at times $t_\Gamma = \frac{\Gamma T}{M}$, where Γ is the image number and M is the number of frames the designer may choose to have between performing the parameter selection process. If desired, the designer can have $M = 1$. The sequence of activities repeats in each such time interval. Note that the time interval need not be between two consecutive frames (in fact, it is not desirable to keep changing the parameter settings in every image).

In many application domains, the above process needs to be implemented in distributed setting. The distributed strategy for collaboration relies on local decision-making at the camera nodes, while being aligned with the suitable global criteria for scene analysis as specified by the user. Some previous work in the multi-agent systems community has shown that this problem has a game-theoretic interpretation, i.e., it can be represented in terms of a cooperative *game* that relies on *multi-player learning and negotiation mechanisms* [Arslan et al., 2007, Fudenberg and Levine, 1998]. This can be done by defining the problem as a cooperative game where the cameras are focused on optimizing their respective local utility functions. If the local utilities can be shown to be aligned with the global utility, then the game can be described as a potential game. However, cameras are directional sensors, targets are dynamic and mapping between targets and cameras is many-to-many. We show later how a game-theoretic strategy can be adapted to solve this problem. The camera parameter selection module attempts to optimize the scene analysis performance at the next imaging time instant, by selecting the camera parameters expected to result in measurements that optimize the criteria specified by the user, such as minimizing the estimated error covariance of the tracker, maximizing the resolution of the targets, minimizing the risk of failing to obtain an image of the target, prioritizing imaging of certain targets dependent on scene information, etc. The network also decides, autonomously, the opportune moments for performing each of these tasks.

5.2   REVIEW OF EXISTING APPROACHES

The issue of integrated sensing and analysis is related to the problem of initial placement of the cameras, which is usually determined at the moment of deployment. Optimal camera placement strategies were proposed in [Zhao et al., 2008] and solved by using a camera placement metric that captures occlusion in 3-D environments. In [Erdem and Sclaroff, 2006], a solution to the problem of optimal camera placement given some coverage constraints was presented and can be used to come up with an initial camera configuration.

The large area covered by these networks results in many situations where observed targets are often not imaged at desirable resolutions. To overcome this issue, the path planning approach proposed by [Qureshi and Terzopoulos, 2009] used a mixed network of cameras. Static cameras were used to track all targets in a virtual environment while PTZ cameras were assigned to obtain high-resolution video from the targets. This approach showed that given the predicted tracks of all the targets, a plan of one-to-one mappings between cameras and targets can be formed to acquire high-resolution videos. A method for determining good sensor configurations that would maximize performance measures was introduced in [Mittal and Davis, 2008]. The configuration framework is based on the presence of random occluding objects and two techniques are proposed to analyze the visibility of the objects. An overview of some main video processing techniques and currents trends for video analysis in PTZ camera networks can be found in [Micheloni et al., 2010]. Most of these methods address the camera network reconfiguration problem in a centralized manner, while a distributed solution is more desirable in many application domains.

A recent distributed approach in [Piciarelli et al., 2009] uses the Expectation-Maximization (EM) algorithm to find the optimal configuration of PTZ cameras given a map of activities. The value of each discretized ground coordinate is determined using the map of activities. This approach upon convergence of the EM algorithm, provides the PTZ settings to optimally cover an area given the map of activities. A framework for distributed control and target assignment in camera networks was presented in [Soto et al., 2009], in which cooperative network control ideas based on multi-player learning in games [Fudenberg and Levine, 1998] were used. The result was a decision making process that aimed to optimize a certain global criterion based on individual decisions by each component (sensor) and the decisions of other interconnected components. The proposed method was related to the vehicle-target assignment problem using game theory as was presented in [Arslan et al., 2007], where a group of vehicles are expected to optimally assign themselves to a set of targets. However, in that work the targets were not dynamic and each vehicle was assigned to one target. In a camera network, each camera can observe multiple targets and multiple cameras can observe each target (many-to-many mapping).

In Table 5.1, we provide a comparison of different methods in the literature that have looked into the problem of camera network control for optimal sensing. We note that they have different

Approach	Objective	Architecture	Outcomes
Mittal and Davis [2008]	Static camera placement	Centralized	Global maxima of area covered while considering occlusion
Soto et al. [2009]	Area coverage	Distributed	Local maxima of total area covered
Piciarelli et al. [2009]	Weighted area coverage based on prior activity map	Distributed	Local maxima of weighted area covered
Qureshi and Terzopoulos [2009]	Camera to target assignment	Centralized	Track based one to one mapping (between cameras and targets) and handoff
Approach in Section 5.3	Satisfies multiple criteria	Distributed	Track based many to many mapping (between cameras and targets)

objective functions, different architectures and different performance criteria. The area of integrated sensing and analysis in camera networks in very much evolving and standard comparison metrics or experimental frameworks are not available. This should be an area of attention as this research matures. In the remainder of this chapter, we will propose a framework for camera network control driven by certain scene understanding criteria. We now explain how the different approaches in the literature are related to this framework.

The method proposed by [Mittal and Davis, 2008] used a simulated annealing approach to evaluate a globally optimal configuration for *static* camera networks. The framework described in Section 5.3 can handle this situation with suitable design of the view utility to model occlusions. The approaches [Piciarelli et al., 2009, Qureshi and Terzopoulos, 2009, Soto et al., 2009] have an independent tracker running in the background. The authors in [Piciarelli et al., 2009] used it to generate the prior (activity map) and then optimize camera settings on the weighed area. In [Qureshi and Terzopoulos, 2009], the authors used tracks to predict the paths of targets to do assignments requiring minimal camera assignment switching, but break when targets mingle due to unreliable predictions. The work in [Soto et al., 2009], while using a distributed tracker, did not tie together the control and tracking modules. The integrated sensing and analysis approach described here is a generalization of all of these and provides a framework for optimizing the image acquisition capabilities based on how well the system objectives are being met. This leads to an optimal allocation of resources and provides overall efficiency to the system. From Figure 5.6 it is seen that in the case where the entire area needs to be covered [Piciarelli et al., 2009, Soto et al., 2009], resources are being used to cover empty space most of the time.

5.3   COLLABORATIVE SENSING IN DISTRIBUTED CAMERA NETWORKS

In this section, we show how to develop a strategy for coordinated control of PTZ camera networks that relies on local decision-making at the camera nodes, while being aligned with the suitable global criteria for scene analysis which are specified by the user. For this purpose, we propose a distributed optimization framework, which can be represented in terms of a cooperative *game* that relies on *multi-*

player learning and negotiation mechanisms [Fudenberg and Levine, 1998]. The result is a decision making process that aims to optimize a certain global criterion based on individual decisions by each component (sensor) and the decisions of other interconnected components. The game theoretic interpretation of this approach is borrowed from previous work on vehicle target assignment problem in cooperative control [Arslan et al., 2007]. We will show how to design specific utility functions and optimization strategies, and provide performance results on real-life camera networks.

5.3.1 SYSTEM MODELING

The position of the i-th camera in the global frame is indicated by $^g\mathbf{p}_i$. In addition to the global frame, each camera defines a frame of reference. The position of T_j in the global frame would be indicated as $^g\mathbf{p}^j$ and in the frame of the i-th camera as $^i\mathbf{p}^j$. The time propagation models for state estimation of T_j are stated below.

Time propagation models

The continuous-time state space model of target T_j is assumed to be

$$\dot{\mathbf{x}}^j(t) = \mathbf{F}\mathbf{x}^j(t) + \mathbf{G}\boldsymbol{\omega}^j(t) , \tag{5.1}$$

where $\mathbf{x}^j = [^g\mathbf{p}^j; {}^g\mathbf{v}^j]$, where $^g\mathbf{p}^j$ and $^g\mathbf{v}^j$ are position and velocity, and $j = 1, \ldots, N_T$ is the target number. The process noise vector $\boldsymbol{\omega}^j \in \Re^3$ is zero mean Gaussian with power spectral density $\mathbf{Q}$. The discrete-time equivalent model is:

$$\mathbf{x}^j(k+1) = \boldsymbol{\Phi}\mathbf{x}^j(k) + \boldsymbol{\gamma}(k) . \tag{5.2}$$

Here, $\boldsymbol{\Phi} = e^{\mathbf{F}T}$, $\boldsymbol{\gamma} \sim \mathcal{N}(\mathbf{0}, \mathbf{Q_d})$, and $T = t_{k+1} - t_k$ is the sampling period. Thus, the state estimate and its error covariance matrix are propagated between sampling instants using

$$\hat{\mathbf{x}}^j(k+1)^- = \boldsymbol{\Phi}\hat{\mathbf{x}}^j(k)^+ \tag{5.3}$$
$$\mathbf{P}^j(k+1)^- = \boldsymbol{\Phi}\mathbf{P}^j(k)^+\boldsymbol{\Phi}^\top + \mathbf{Q}_d . \tag{5.4}$$

Coordinate Transformations

Target T_j's position in the i-th camera frame is related to its position in the global frame by

$$^g\mathbf{p}^j = {}^g_i\mathbf{R}\,{}^i\mathbf{p}^j + {}^g\mathbf{p}_i \tag{5.5}$$
$$^i\mathbf{p}^j = {}^i_g\mathbf{R}[^g\mathbf{p}^j - {}^g\mathbf{p}_i] , \tag{5.6}$$

where $^i_g\mathbf{R}$ is a rotation matrix that is a function of the camera mounting angle, the pan angle, and the tilt angle.

Measurement Model

This section presents the nonlinear and linearized measurement models for target T_j when imaged by camera i. The linearization is performed relative to the targets estimated position $^g\hat{\mathbf{p}}^j$. In the remainder of this section, all measurement vectors are computed at t_k. The time argument and subscripts are dropped to simplify the notation where understanding of the material is not compromised.

We assume that positions ${}^g\hat{\mathbf{p}}^j$ and ${}^g\mathbf{p}_i$ are known, that the rotation matrix ${}^i_g\mathbf{R}(\rho_i, \tau_i)$ is a known function of the pan and the tilt angles, and that the focal length F_i is a known function of the zoom setting ζ_i. Let the coordinates of target T_j in the i-th camera frame be ${}^i\mathbf{p}^j = \begin{bmatrix} {}^ix^j, {}^iy^j, {}^iz^j \end{bmatrix}^\top$. Using the standard pin-hole camera model with perspective projection, the projection of ${}^i\mathbf{p}^j$ onto the image plane of camera i is ${}^i\mathbf{u}^j = \begin{bmatrix} F_i \frac{{}^ix^j}{{}^iz^j}, & F_i \frac{{}^iy^j}{{}^iz^j}, & F_i \end{bmatrix}^\top$. Thus, the image plane measurement ${}^i\mathbf{u}^j$ is

$$
{}^i\mathbf{u}^j = \begin{bmatrix} F_i \frac{{}^ix^j}{{}^iz^j} \\ F_i \frac{{}^iy^j}{{}^iz^j} \end{bmatrix} + {}^i\boldsymbol{\eta}^j, \tag{5.7}
$$

where the measurement noise ${}^i\boldsymbol{\eta}^j \sim \mathcal{N}(\mathbf{0}, \mathbf{C}_i^j)$ with $\mathbf{C}_i^j > \mathbf{0}$ and $\mathbf{C}_i^j \in \mathfrak{R}^{2\times2}$.

Given the estimated state and the camera model, the predicted estimate of the measurement is

$$
{}^i\hat{\mathbf{u}}^j = \begin{bmatrix} F_i \frac{{}^i\hat{x}^j}{{}^i\hat{z}^j} \\ F_i \frac{{}^i\hat{y}^j}{{}^i\hat{z}^j} \end{bmatrix}. \tag{5.8}
$$

The measurement residual ${}^i\tilde{\mathbf{u}}^j$ is defined as

$$
{}^i\tilde{\mathbf{u}}^j = {}^i\mathbf{u}^j - {}^i\hat{\mathbf{u}}^j. \tag{5.9}
$$

Observation Matrix $\mathbf{H}_i^j$

Given ${}^g\mathbf{p}_i$, ${}^g\hat{\mathbf{p}}^j$, and ${}^i_g\mathbf{R}$, subsequent analysis will use the linearized relationship by the first order Taylor series expansion of eqn. (5.7) around the estimated state. The linear relationship between the residual and the state error vector is

$$
{}^i\mathbf{u}^j - {}^i\hat{\mathbf{u}}^j \approx \mathbf{H}_i^j ({}^g\mathbf{p}^j - {}^g\hat{\mathbf{p}}^j), \tag{5.10}
$$

where $\mathbf{H}_i^j = \frac{\partial {}^i\mathbf{u}^j}{\partial {}^g\mathbf{p}^j}\Big|_{{}^g\hat{\mathbf{p}}^j} \in \mathfrak{R}^{2\times3}$. Taking the partial derivatives as defined above, it is straightforward to show that

$$
\mathbf{H}_i^j = \frac{F_i}{({}^i\hat{z}^j)^2} \begin{bmatrix} {}^g\mathbf{N}_1^{j\top} \\ {}^g\mathbf{N}_2^{j\top} \end{bmatrix}, \tag{5.11}
$$

where

$$
{}^g\mathbf{N}_1^j = {}^g_i\mathbf{R}\,{}^i\mathbf{N}_1^j \qquad {}^i\mathbf{N}_1^j = \begin{bmatrix} {}^i\hat{z}^j, 0, -{}^i\hat{x}^j \end{bmatrix}^\top
$$
$$
{}^g\mathbf{N}_2^j = {}^g_i\mathbf{R}\,{}^i\mathbf{N}_2^j \qquad {}^i\mathbf{N}_2^j = \begin{bmatrix} 0, {}^i\hat{z}^j, -{}^i\hat{y}^j \end{bmatrix}^\top
$$

are the vectors normal to the vector from camera i's origin to the j-th target's estimated position $^i\hat{\mathbf{p}}^j$. Let us define matrix $^g\mathbf{N}^{j^\top}$ as follows:

$$^g\mathbf{N}^{j^\top} = \begin{bmatrix} ^g\mathbf{N}_1^{j^\top} \\ ^g\mathbf{N}_2^{j^\top} \end{bmatrix}. \qquad (5.12)$$

Thus, the observation matrix can be written as

$$\mathbf{H}_i^j = \frac{F_i}{(^i\hat{z}^j)^2} {}^g\mathbf{N}^{j^\top}. \qquad (5.13)$$

5.3.2 DISTRIBUTED OPTIMIZATION FRAMEWORK

The objective of the team of cameras is to optimize a global utility function, $U_G(\mathbf{a})$. For it to be solved in a distributed environment, $U_G(\mathbf{a})$ must be converted into smaller local utilities, $U_{C_i}(\mathbf{a})$, for each camera. We assume that each camera is a rational decision maker that optimizes its own utility function, thus indirectly translating to the optimization of a global utility function. Convergence requires the local camera utilities to be aligned with the global utility. This implies that a change in the camera utility, $U_{C_i}(\mathbf{a})$, affects the global utility $U_G(\mathbf{a})$ similarly. As shown in [Monderer and Shapley, 1996], this representation leads to a potential game that uses the global utility as an potential function.

A game is called a **potential game** if the incentive of all players to change the strategy can be expressed in a global potential function [Monderer and Shapley, 1996]. This concept of potentiality helps us to specify an important set of games because of their desirable convergence properties. If $\mathbf{a} \in S$, where S is the collection of all possible camera parameter settings in the game G, then the global utility function $U_G(\mathbf{a}) : \mathbf{S} \to \Re$ is an ordinal potential function for the game G, if $\forall \mathbf{a} \in S$ and $\forall \mathbf{a}_i, \mathbf{b}_i \in S_i$,

$$\left(U_{C_i}(\mathbf{b}_i, \mathbf{a}_{-i}) - U_{C_i}(\mathbf{a}_i, \mathbf{a}_{-i}) > 0\right) \Rightarrow \left(U_G(\mathbf{b}_i, \mathbf{a}_{-i}) - U_G(\mathbf{a}_i, \mathbf{a}_{-i}) > 0\right), \qquad (5.14)$$

where $\Delta U_{C_i}(\mathbf{a}) > 0$ makes the game a maximum game. This allows us to maximize the global utility through the maximization of the utility of each camera. This can be achieved by making the camera utility equivalent to its contribution to the global utility.

Let S_i be the set of all the possible camera setting profiles for C_i. Let $\Delta U_{C_i}(\mathbf{a})$ be the change in camera utility caused by the change in camera parameters settings from setting $\mathbf{a}_i$ to setting $\mathbf{b}_i$, such that $\mathbf{a}_i, \mathbf{b}_i \in S_i$. Then, if

$$\Delta U_{C_i}(\mathbf{a}) = \left(U_{C_i}(\mathbf{b}_i, \mathbf{a}_{-i}) - U_{C_i}(\mathbf{a}_i, \mathbf{a}_{-i})\right) > 0, \qquad (5.15)$$

the resultant change in the global utility $\Delta U_G(\mathbf{a})$ caused by the change in parameters is

$$\Delta U_G(\mathbf{a}) = \left(U_G(\mathbf{b}_i, \mathbf{a}_{-i}) - U_G(\mathbf{a}_i, \mathbf{a}_{-i})\right) > 0. \qquad (5.16)$$

Hence, for change in camera parameter settings in a single camera, we conclude,

$$\Delta U_{C_i}(\mathbf{a}) > 0 \Rightarrow \Delta U_G(\mathbf{a}) > 0. \qquad (5.17)$$

A well-known concept in game theory is the notion of Nash equilibrium. In the context of our image network problem, it will be defined as a choice of parameter settings $a^* = (a_1^*, ..., a_{N_c}^*)$ such that no sensor could improve its utility further by deviating from a^*, i.e., by choosing a different set of parameters, the utility functions of all cameras cannot be improved further as expressed in (5.18) below. Obviously, this is a function of time since the targets are dynamic and the cameras could also be mobile or capable of panning, tilting and zooming. For example, for the problem of tracking all targets, a Nash equilibrium may be reached at a particular instant of time when all the cameras are collectively observing all the targets in the deployment region at an acceptable resolution and there is no advantage for a particular camera to choose some other target to observe. Mathematically, if a_{-i} denotes the collection of parameter settings of all cameras *except* camera C_i, then a^* is a *pure Nash equilibrium* if

$$U_{C_i}(a_i^*, a_{-i}^*) = \max_{a_i \in \mathcal{A}_i} U_{C_i}(a_i, a_{-i}^*), \forall C_i \in \mathcal{C}. \qquad (5.18)$$

By defining the global utility function as the ordinal potential function, with the individual local camera utilities aligned to it, the game becomes a potential game. If a game has a continuous ordinal potential function, then the game has at least one Nash Equilibrium. Therefore, if the camera network has an arbitrary initial camera settings profile **a**, then at each step, one camera increases its own utility. Similarly, as seen in Eqn. (5.17), the global utility increases by $\Delta U_G(\mathbf{a}) > 0$ at each step. Since, $U_G(\mathbf{a})$ can only accept a finite number of values, it will eventually reach a local maxima. At this point, no camera can achieve further improvement and thus a Nash equilibrium is reached.

Game theory has been shown to be a powerful tool for the design and control of multi-agent system [Campos-Nanez et al., 2008, Scutari et al., 2009]. As explained in [Li and Marden, 2011], the design of multi-agent systems can be thought of a concatenation between a designed game and a distributed learning algorithm and parallels the theme of distributed optimization. Game theory-based camera network design/control approaches focus on the decomposition of the global mission objective to local agent objective functions at each of the cameras. A distributed learning scheme, Spatial Adaptive Play (SAP) [Young, 1998], for potential games is then utilized to guarantee convergence to a Nash equilibrium

5.3.3   CHOICE OF UTILITY FUNCTIONS

To implement the above framework, we need to design utility functions that reflect the scene understanding criteria. The set of criteria that the camera network must satisfy is modeled using the global utility function $U_G(\mathbf{a})$, where $\mathbf{a} = (a_1, ..., a_{N_c})$ denotes the collection of parameter settings for all cameras. In almost every task, the specified criteria is directly associated with the targets, e.g., getting shots at desired resolution and pose. We can assign a target utility, $U_T(\mathbf{a})$, that defines the satisfaction of the criteria, given parameter settings **a**, for a target. The maximization of the utility functions across all targets, constrained by the parameter sets of the camera network, results in the set of parameters that best satisfies the criteria at some point in time.

Target Utility

Assuming there are L criteria that the camera network needs to meet, the satisfaction of those criteria on a target T_j is measured by a set of metrics $\{M_1(\mathbf{a}, T_j), ..., M_L(\mathbf{a}, T_j)\}$, which are functions of parameter settings for all cameras. The target utility describes the set of criteria for target T_j, which can be represented as a function of the set of metrics on T_j, i.e.,

$$U_{T_j}(\mathbf{a}) = \mathcal{F}(M_1(\mathbf{a}, T_j), ..., M_L(\mathbf{a}, T_j)). \tag{5.19}$$

There could be many choices of $\mathcal{F}(\cdot)$, one possible form of $\mathcal{F}$ being weighted summation, i.e.,

$$U_{T_j}(\mathbf{a}) = w_1 \cdot M_1(\mathbf{a}, T_j) + ... + w_L \cdot M_L(\mathbf{a}, T_j). \tag{5.20}$$

The weights preceding each metric define the relevance/importance of each criterion and can be dynamically modified to allow for fine grain control of the behavior of the camera network towards each target T_j. The higher the weight, the greater the emphasis of the corresponding criterion. A sample set of possible utility functions for different criteria is given below.

a) Tracking Criterion

The purpose of the tracking utility is to quantify how well the tracking module in camera C_i is tracking target T_j given the settings a_i. Let $M_{Tr}(\mathbf{a}, T_j)$ denote the tracking utility of T_j, it can be formulated via the Fisher Information matrix, will be monotonically increasing with the tracking accuracy of the target that is least accurately tracked.

Fisher Information J

When the target state estimation process completes at t_δ, a prior position estimate ${}^g\hat{\mathbf{p}}^j(k+1)^-$ is available for the j-th target at the future image sample time t_{k+1}, along with a prior covariance matrix $\mathbf{P}^j(k+1)^-$. In the remainder of this section, all covariance and information matrices are computed at t_{k+1}. The time argument is dropped to simplify the notation. The posterior information matrix is denoted as $\mathbf{J}^{j+} = \left(\mathbf{P}^{j+}\right)^{-1}$ which is a function of the camera settings $\mathbf{a}$:

$$\mathbf{J}^{j+} = \mathbf{J}^{j-} + \sum_{i=1}^{N_C} \mathbf{H}_i^{j\top} \left(\mathbf{C}_i^j\right)^{-1} \mathbf{H}_i^j \tag{5.21}$$

because each $\mathbf{H}_i^j$ is a function of $\mathbf{a}_i$, as was shown in Section 5.3.1. Note also that, through $\mathbf{H}_i^j$, the posterior information is a function of the target position which is a random variable ${}^g\mathbf{p}^j \sim \mathcal{N}({}^g\hat{\mathbf{p}}^j, \mathbf{P}^{j-})$; therefore, $\mathbf{J}^{j+}$ is a random variable. Finally, note that $\mathbf{C}_i^j$ is finite only when T_j is within the field-of-view of C_i; otherwise, the corresponding term of the summation has value zero. Eqn. (5.21) can be decomposed as

$$\mathbf{J}^{j+} = \left(\mathbf{J}^{j-} + \mathbf{H}_{-i}^{j\top} \left(\mathbf{C}_{-i}^j\right)^{-1} \mathbf{H}_{-i}^j\right) + \mathbf{H}_i^{j\top} \left(\mathbf{C}_i^j\right)^{-1} \mathbf{H}_i^j.$$

This decomposition is convenient for decentralized optimization, because while C_i is optimizing its parameters $\mathbf{a}_i$, the contribution from prior information and all other cameras is constant.

Note that in all summations in this section the information $\mathbf{H}_i^{j\top}\left(\mathbf{C}_i^j\right)^{-1}\mathbf{H}_i^j$ for T_j from C_i is only actually received if the actual position of T_j at the time of the next image is within the field-of-view (FOV) of C_i in the next image. The parameter settings $\mathbf{a}$ determine the Fisher information and the FOV for each camera. In the subsequent sections, the phrase "if in FOV" will be used to succinctly indicate this fact.

The posterior Information matrix for the j-th target $\mathbf{J}^{j+}$ can be represented in block form as

$$\mathbf{J}^{j+} = \begin{bmatrix} \mathbf{J}_{pp}^{j+} & \mathbf{J}_{pv}^{j+} \\ \mathbf{J}_{vp}^{j+} & \mathbf{J}_{vv}^{j+} \end{bmatrix}, \tag{5.22}$$

where $\mathbf{J}_{pp}^{j+}$ represents the position information matrix. Using Singular Value Decomposition, $\mathbf{J}_{pp}^{j+}$ can be factored as

$$\mathbf{J}_{pp}^{j+} = \mathbf{M}^j \mathbf{\Sigma}^j \mathbf{M}^{j\top} \tag{5.23}$$

$$= \begin{bmatrix} \mathbf{m}_1^j & \mathbf{m}_2^j \end{bmatrix} \begin{bmatrix} \sigma_1^j & 0 \\ 0 & \sigma_2^j \end{bmatrix} \begin{bmatrix} (\mathbf{m}_1^j)^\top \\ (\mathbf{m}_2^j)^\top \end{bmatrix}. \tag{5.24}$$

In this factorization, $\mathbf{m}_1^j$ and $\mathbf{m}_2^j$ are orthonormal *information* vectors and σ_1^j and σ_2^j are the information in the directions of $\mathbf{m}_1^j$ and $\mathbf{m}_2^j$, respectively.

Let us define $J(\mathbf{a})$ such that,

$$J^j(\mathbf{a}) = \min\left(\sigma_1^j, \sigma_2^j\right). \tag{5.25}$$

J^j represents the accuracy of tracking T_j using Extended Kalman-Consensus Filter (see Section 3.3.2 and [Song et al., 2010b]), thus it can be used to define the tracking utility of T_j, i.e.,

$$M_{Tr}(\mathbf{a}, T_j) = J^j(\mathbf{a}). \tag{5.26}$$

The parameter settings $\mathbf{a}$ determine the Fisher information and the FOV for each camera.

b) Imaging Criterion

The imaging utility $M_I(\mathbf{a}, T_j)$ determines whether the resolution and/or pose requirement of target T_j is satisfied by the camera network using settings profile $\mathbf{a}$. Thus, the imaging utility will comprise of a viewing angle coefficient and a resolution coefficient.

Let T_j maneuver in the area with a direction vector $\vec{O}_{T_j}$. Defining a vector $\vec{O}_{C_i}$ from camera C_i's position ${}^g\mathbf{p}_i$ to T_j's estimated position ${}^g\hat{\mathbf{p}}^j$, we can compute the view angle θ_i^j formed by T_j at C_i as,

$$\theta_i^j = \arccos\left(\frac{\vec{O}_{T_j} \cdot \vec{O}_{C_i}}{\|\vec{O}_{T_j}\| \|\vec{O}_{C_i}\|}\right). \tag{5.27}$$

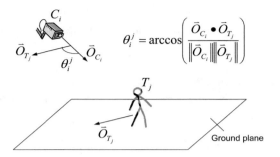

Figure 5.3: Camera viewing angle and Target pose.

An illustration of the view angle factor is shown in Figure 5.3.

In many instances, only one high-resolution image per target may be required. Once one such image is acquired for T_j, then the utility contributed by the imaging utility should have added value only if a high-resolution image can be procured at a new viewing angle θ_i^{jn} that is closer to the desired view angle $\bar{\theta}^j$, or at a higher resolution, or both.

Let us assume that at a previous time, a high-resolution image of T_j was obtained at viewing angle θ^{jp}. Let θ_i^{jn} be the angle at which camera C_i can procure a new image of T_j.

Defining a view angle coefficient m_i^θ that weighs $M_{I_j}(\mathbf{a})$ to provide a higher value for a new viewing angle θ_i^{jn} closer to the desired angle $\bar{\theta}^j$ than the previous viewing angle θ^{jp},

$$
m_i^\theta = \begin{cases} 1 - \dfrac{|\bar{\theta}^j - \theta_i^{jn}|}{|\bar{\theta}^j - \theta^{jp}|} & \text{if } |\bar{\theta}^j - \theta_i^{jp}| > |\bar{\theta}^j - \theta^{jn}| \\ 0 & \text{otherwise} \end{cases} . \tag{5.28}
$$

Assuming that the target is facing in the direction of motion, the $|\cdot|$ in Eqn. (5.28) provides a positive non-zero value of m_i^θ, only when targets are moving towards the camera. Thus, the scalar m_i^θ measures alignment of the camera-to-target vector with the target's direction vector.

This leads us to defining a resolution coefficient m_i^r as a measure of viewing target T_j at a desired resolution $\bar{r}$.

$$
m_i^r = \begin{cases} \dfrac{r_i^j - \underline{r}}{\bar{r} - \underline{r}} & \text{if } \underline{r} \leq r_i^j \leq \bar{r} \\ 0 & \text{otherwise} \end{cases} , \tag{5.29}
$$

where $\underline{r}$ and $\bar{r}$ are the minimum and maximum height requirements of target T_j in the camera image plane, and r_i^j is the resolution at which T_j is being viewed at by C_i.

Thus, we can now define an imaging utility $M_I(\mathbf{a}, T_j)$ for a given pose and resolution requirement as:

$$
M_I(\mathbf{a}, T_j) = \max_i \left(m_i^\theta m_i^r \right) . \tag{5.30}
$$

This utility prioritizes certain poses or facial shots by factoring in viewing angle and resolution, and then picks a camera C_i from the available N_C cameras, that provides maximum imaging utility.

Global Utility

The global utility, U_G, describes the desirability of the settings profile $\mathbf{a}$, given the criteria that must be satisfied by the camera network. This is represented as a function of the importance/priority of each target T_j and its related target utility U_T. Thus,

$$U_G(\mathbf{a}) = v_1 \cdot U_{T_1}(\mathbf{a}) + ... + v_{N_T} \cdot U_{T_{N_T}}(\mathbf{a}) , \qquad (5.31)$$

where v_j denotes the importance of target T_j. By maximizing the global utility, we are choosing the settings profile that best satisfies the criteria specified for the camera network.

The global utility is dependent on the estimated position of the target which is a random variable. Therefore, it may be necessary to consider the expected value of the global utility function over the distribution of the uncertainty in the estimated position of the target, as explained later in Section 5.4.1.

Camera Utility

The global utilities must now be converted into smaller local utilities in order for them to be solved in a distributed fashion. Convergence proofs in game theory [Monderer and Shapley, 1996] require that the local utilities are aligned with the global utility, i.e., a change in the local utility affects the global utility similarly. We achieve this by making the utility of our camera equivalent to its contribution to the global utility, i.e.,

$$U_{C_i}(\mathbf{a}) = U_G(\mathbf{a}) - U_G(\mathbf{a}_{-i}), \qquad (5.32)$$

where the set $\mathbf{a}_{-i}$ is the set of settings profiles excluding the profile for camera i. This is known as the Wonderful Life Utility (WLU) [Wolpert and Tumor, 2004], and as shown in [Monderer and Shapley, 1996] and applied in [Arslan et al., 2007], leads to a potential game using the global utility as the potential function. This allows us to maximize the global utility through the maximization of the utility of each camera.

5.3.4   NEGOTIATION MECHANISMS

The dynamic nature of the region being observed requires that our cameras communicate with each other in order to decide the set of parameters that will result in the optimal global utility. Each camera negotiates with the other cameras to accurately predict the actions of the other cameras before deciding its own action [Monderer and Shapley, 1996].

The overall idea of the proposed negotiation strategy is to use *learning algorithms for multi-player games* [Monderer and Shapley, 1996]. A particularly appealing strategy for this problem is Spatial Adaptive Play (SAP) [Young, 1998]. This is because it can be implemented with a low computational burden on each camera and leads to an optimal assignment of targets with arbitrarily high probabilities for the WLU described above. In a particular step of the SAP negotiation strategy, a camera is chosen randomly according to a uniform distribution. This camera can update its parameter settings so as to maximize its own utility by taking into account the proposed parameter settings of all the other cameras in the previous step.

Application of SAP Negotiation Mechanism:
At any step of SAP negotiations, a camera C_i is randomly chosen from the pool of cameras in the network according to a uniform distribution over the cameras, and only this camera is given the chance to update its proposed parameter settings. At negotiation step k, C_i proposes a parameter setting according to the following probability distribution based on other cameras' parameters at the previous step:

$$p_i(k) = \sigma \left(\frac{1}{\tau} \begin{bmatrix} U_{C_i}(A_i^1, \mathbf{a}_{-i}(k-1)) \\ \vdots \\ U_{C_i}(A_i^{|\mathcal{A}_i|}, \mathbf{a}_{-i}(k-1)) \end{bmatrix} \right) \tag{5.33}$$

for some $\tau > 0$, where $a(k-1)$ denotes the profile of proposed parameter settings at step $k-1$, $\mathcal{A}_i = \{A_i^1, ..., A_i^{|\mathcal{A}_i|}\}$ is the enumeration of all possible parameter settings of camera C_i, and $|\mathcal{A}_i|$ is the number of elements in $\mathcal{A}_i$. $\sigma(.)$ is the logit or soft-max function, and its mth element is defined as

$$(\sigma(x))_m = \frac{e^{x_m}}{e^{x_1} + \cdots + e^{x_n}}.$$

The constant τ determines how likely C_i is to select a parameter setting. If $\tau \to \infty$, C_i will select any setting $a_i \in \mathcal{A}_i$ with equal probability. As $\tau \to 0$, C_i will select a setting from its best response set as

$$\{a_i \in \mathcal{A}_i : U_{C_i}(a_i, \mathbf{a}_{-i}(t-1)) = \max_{a_i' \in \mathcal{A}_i} U_{C_i}(a_i', \mathbf{a}_{-i}(t-1))\}$$

with probability close to 1. In our implementation, we let $\tau \to 0$. After C_i updates its settings, it broadcasts its parameters (i.e., pan, tilt and zoom) to all neighboring cameras. The other cameras can then use that information to update their parameters after being chosen at any negotiation step until a consensus is reached. This occurs when the cameras have reached an Nash equilibrium, i.e., when no camera can increase the global utility by changing its parameters.

The utility functions combined with the negotiation strategy guarantees that at each time step the set of parameters chosen for the network of cameras is an optimal solution for the system's goals as defined by the global utility. In practice, we will not need to do this at every time step. The optimization can be done whenever the utility falls below a certain threshold.

5.3.5   EXAMPLE SCENARIOS

In this section, we will demonstrate how to apply the above principles in real life application scenarios by designing utility functions that are tied to various scene understanding criteria. Consider a network of N_C PTZ smart cameras each of which has the ability to perform person detection, tracking and some high level processing tasks, as needed by the application (e.g., recognition of basic activities).

Example 1 - Cover entire area with at least some minimum resolution while focusing on some targets at higher resolution

To cover the entire area, the area can be divided into grids in a way similar to [Erdem and Sclaroff, 2006] to make the problem more tractable. Then each grid of the area is treated as a virtual target. Since the goal is covering entire area at a required resolution, there is no risk of losing a target if the goal is achieved. Thus, only the imaging utility needs to be considered in this case. As view angle does not need to be considered for empty area, for a virtual target T_j^v, (5.30) is modified as $M_I(\mathbf{a}, T_j^v) = \max_i (m_i^r)$ by setting m_i^θ to be a constant "1", such that the utility of T_j^v is

$$U_{T_j^v}(\mathbf{a}) = M_I(\mathbf{a}, T_j^v) \text{ with } \underline{r} = r_v, \quad \text{for } j = 1, ..., N_g, \tag{5.34}$$

where N_g is the total number of grid cells, m_i^r is defined in (5.29), $\underline{r}$ is the minimum resolution and r_v is the minimum requirement for covering the entire area as specified by an application/user.

For some user specified real targets that need to be viewed with higher resolution, although a tracking module is run on them to provide the estimates of their positions, we do not factor the tracking performance into the optimization function because the entire area is required to be covered. This is similar to [Soto et al., 2009]. We refer to this case as the **Area Coverage** problem. The utilities for those specified real targets are

$$U_{T_j^h}(\mathbf{a}) = M_I(\mathbf{a}, T_j^h) \text{ with } \underline{r} = r_h, \quad \text{for } j = N_g + 1, ..., N_g + N_T, \tag{5.35}$$

where $M_I(\mathbf{a}, T_j^h)$ is the imaging utility defined in (5.30) and r_h is the resolution requirement for those specified targets. Now we can define the global utility as

$$U_G(\mathbf{a}) = v^h \sum_{j=N_g+1}^{N_g+N_T} U_{T_j^h}(\mathbf{a}) + v^v \sum_{j=1}^{N_g} U_{T_j^v}(\mathbf{a}), \tag{5.36}$$

where N_T is the number of user specified targets and the importance of those high-resolution targets, v^h, should be set to be higher than that of virtual targets, v^v.

Example 2 - Cover entrances of area while optimizing tracking of targets within area

The purpose of the system here is to minimize the tracking error of all targets within the region under surveillance and obtain the best possible shots for each target. The choice of camera parameters determines the expected assignment of targets to cameras, as well as the expected tracking accuracy and risk. Given that the targets are moving, when the entire area is not covered, there is a tradeoff between tracking gain and coverage risk. Each camera may view only a portion of the area under surveillance. Here we also consider the issue that the importance of every location within the observed space may not be equal. Monitoring entrances and exits to the area under consideration will allow us to identify, and subsequently track all targets, whereas monitoring empty space is of little use.

To achieve the system goal, the camera control is aware of the state of the Kalman-Consensus filter and actively seeks to provide it with the most informative measurements for state estimation, which makes the architecture of the system in this case different from the Area Coverage one in Example 1. Furthermore, the estimated error covariance is considered in addition to the estimated state of each target. This allows the optimization to gauge the risk of failing to capture a feature when attempting high-resolution shots. We refer to this case as the ***Target Coverage*** problem.

From the tracking and imaging metrics defined in (5.26) and (5.30), we can define the target utility as the metrics generated by viewing target T_j, or

$$U_{T_j}(\mathbf{a}) = w_1^j M_{Tr}(\mathbf{a}, T_j) + w_2^j M_I(\mathbf{a}, T_j) , \qquad (5.37)$$

where w_1^j and w_2^j are the weights corresponding to the tracking metric and view metric for target T_j. We can then determine those settings profiles that maximize the global utility based on analysis of $U_G(\mathbf{a})$.

By setting a higher value for w_2^j (compared to w_1^j), the camera network will attempt to acquire a high resolution shot of the target j. This has the added effect of reducing overlap within the fields of view of the network. The estimated error covariance of a target grows the longer a target is not observed. The larger the estimated error covariance, the larger the area that needs to be covered to decrease the risk of losing a target. Thus, the system will prefer a setting whereby a larger area will be covered so that the lost target can be imaged, even through this camera will be at low resolution.

Example 3 - Cover entire area with at least some minimum resolution while optimizing tracking of targets within area

This case is a combination of the Area Coverage and Target Coverage problems. From Examples 1 and 2, we can easily define the global utility as

$$U_G(\mathbf{a}) = \sum_{j=N_g+1}^{N_g+N_T} v_j^h \left(w_1^j M_{Tr}(\mathbf{a}, T_j^h) + w_2^j M_I(\mathbf{a}, T_j^h) \right) + v^v \sum_{j=1}^{N_g} M_I(\mathbf{a}, T_j^v). \qquad (5.38)$$

5.3.6   RESULTS IN EXAMPLE SCENARIOS

Area Coverage

We show example results on a real-life camera network. The sensor network consists of 9 PTZ cameras with a resolution of 320×240 pixels. We use this setting to show the performance of our approach with the increasing number of zooming cameras.

Figure 5.4 demonstrates the ability of the game theoretic approach to self-organize to maintain coverage while allowing some cameras to zoom in for high-resolution images. Figure 5.4 (a) shows the initial convergence result that covers the entire area at an acceptable resolution. The coverage is shown on the bottom-right (blue areas are covered, white areas are not; the darker the color of a block, the greater the number of cameras that are assigned there). Figure 5.4 (b) shows that when one camera zooms in (camera C_8, bounded with red lines) the other cameras automatically adjust their settings (camera C_5 zooms out) to keep the area covered. Figure 5.4 (c)-(e) show the affect of increasing the number of cameras zooming in from 2 to 4. It is seen that as the number of zoomed in cameras increases, more areas are left uncovered. Figure 5.4 (f) shows the re-initialization result when we reset the cameras with none of them zooming in - the network of cameras can again keep the entire area covered. By comparing 5.4 (f) with (a), it can be noticed that the parameter settings in (f) are different with those in (a), although both of them could satisfy the coverage requirements. This illustrates that the Nash equilibrium is not unique.

Target Coverage

First, we show results on a real-life camera network, and then compare with the design for Area Coverage of Example 1. For the following experiments the tracking and view utilities were weighted high with risk weighted low.

Our camera network is composed of 5 PTZ cameras surrounding a 600 m^2 courtyard. The area was divided into a number of grids, each of size 1cm^2. Tracked targets were assumed to have a height of 1.80 m. Each camera acquires images of resolution 640 × 480 pixels. Thus, r_i^j is the largest number of pixels in the vertical direction occupied by T_j in the image plane of some camera in the network. The cameras were arranged such that 4 of the cameras were located on the same side of the courtyard, with one camera on the opposite side. In the region of interest there were 5 targets in addition to two entrances and exits. Since the entrances and exits must be monitored always, we treated them as static virtual targets, leading to a total of 7 targets. Each camera in our setup is an independent entity connected through a wireless network, with the entire system running in real time.

At initialization, all of the cameras apply the utility function defined in Section 5.3.5 for the Area Coverage to cover the entire region under surveillance and to detect targets already in the region. The target detection modules in each camera determine the image plane position of each target in its field of view. This information is then passed along to the Extended Kalman-Consensus filter and is processed along with the information from the filters running on neighboring cameras as described in Section 3.3.2.

We compare two scenarios: Area Coverage and Target Coverage. In the Area Coverage problem, the camera networks has to cover the entire area and take shots at lower resolutions, resulting in increased tracking error. We will show the results for both the Area Coverage and Target Coverage system (where only targets and entrances are covered), and clearly show the advantages of optimizing the tracking within the control module. The targets followed the same path through the courtyard during the collection of data for both cases. Figure 5.5 shows the images captured by the actively controlled camera network at different time steps. Figure 5.5(a) shows the result for the Area Coverage as the initialization. Figure 5.5(b)-(d) show the results for the Target Coverage. Since targets are

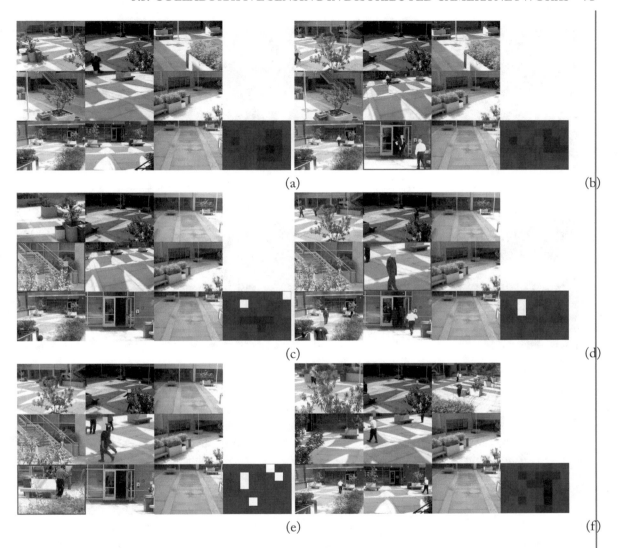

Figure 5.4: Results of game theoretic camera control with the number of cameras that zoom in increasing. The coverage of the entire space is shown on the right-bottom of each sub-figure, where blue areas are covered, white areas are not. The darker the color of a block, the greater the number of cameras that are assigned there. The results with multiple cameras zooming in are showed in (b)–(e). The number of cameras that zoom in is increasing from 1 to 4. From (b)–(e), the view of new zooming in camera is bounded by red lines. It is seen that as the number of zoomed in cameras increases, more areas are left uncovered. (f) shows the re-initialization results when we reset the cameras with none of them zooming in. (From [Song et al., 2011b]).

(a) Time Step $k = 0$

(b) Time Step $k = 2$

(c) Time Step $k = 19$

(d) Time Step $k = 36$

Figure 5.5: Dynamic camera control images. Blue regions mark the field of view, lighter regions identify camera overlap. Targets are marked in green with red label. This figure is best viewed on a computer monitor. (From [Song et al., 2011a])

free to move about the region under surveillance, the cameras in the network are required to adjust their parameters dynamically to maintain shots of each target that optimize the utility functions presented in Section 5.3.5. To acquire these shots the camera network concedes a large unobserved area. We can see in Figure 5.6 that as time progresses, the average trace of the covariance and the resolution of all targets settle at a significantly better value (compared to the Area Coverage) when the tracking and control modules are integrated together (as proposed in this paper). This is because at each time step the camera network will choose the set of parameters that optimizes the utility, which is dependent on the error covariance of the Extended Kalman-Consensus filter.

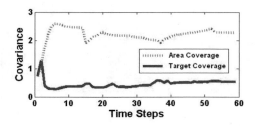
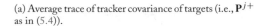

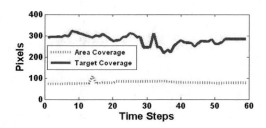

(a) Average trace of tracker covariance of targets (i.e., $\mathbf{P}^{j+}$ as in (5.4)).

(b) Average resolution of targets over time (i.e., r_i^j as in (5.29)).

Figure 5.6: Comparison of the average tracker covariance and average resolution of all targets being actively tracked by a system for Target Coverage vs. one for Area Coverage. (From [Song et al., 2011a])

5.4   OPPORTUNISTIC SENSING

The goal of opportunistic sensing is to collaboratively control the cameras for optimal tracking , while making provision for opportunistic high-resolution imagery at desired poses for targets spread in wide-area environments. However, high-resolution imagery comes at a higher risk of losing the target in a dynamic environment due to the corresponding decrease in the FOV. Therefore, we further define a Bayesian value function $V(\mathbf{a})$ as the expected value of the global utility function, which incorporates the risk of losing track on a target. The maximization of the value function across all targets, constrained by the parameter sets of the camera network, results in the set of parameters that best satisfies the criteria at some point in time.

5.4.1   GLOBAL UTILITY

In our design, the global utility function should first ensure that all targets are tracked at all times, while encouraging high-resolution imagery at instants of time when they are possible without sacrificing the tracking specification. Thus, we define the global utility $U_G(\mathbf{a})$ as the sum of the utilities generated by viewing all targets, but by conditioning it on factors like, how well targets are being tracked, when is the opportune time to image targets at a high resolution, and at what pose, i.e.,

$$U_G(\mathbf{a}) = U_{Tr}(\mathbf{a}) + \sum_{j=1}^{N_T} \left(v_j \left(g\left(U_{Tr}\right) + f(d^{jj'}) \right) M_I(\mathbf{a}, T_j) \right), \qquad (5.39)$$

where $U_{Tr}(\mathbf{a}) = \min_j M_{Tr}(\mathbf{a}, T_j)$ represents the least tracking accuracy over all targets, $M_{Tr}(\mathbf{a}, T_j)$ and $M_I(\mathbf{a}, T_j)$ are the tracking and imaging utility defined in (5.26) and (5.30), respectively. v_j is a possibly time varying weight that magnifies the importance of imagery for certain targets relative to others, g and f are continuously differentiable monotonically increasing bounded functions.

The function $g\left(U_{Tr}\right)$ is defined as

$$g\left(U_{Tr}\right) = \frac{1}{1 + \exp\left(\kappa_g\left(\bar{P} - U_{Tr}\right)\right)} \tag{5.40}$$

and the function $f(d^{jj'})$ is defined as

$$f(d^{jj'}) = \frac{1}{1 + \exp\left(\kappa_f\left(d^{jj'} - \bar{d}^j\right)\right)}, \tag{5.41}$$

where $\bar{P}$ is the tracking accuracy threshold and the scalar $d^{jj'}$ is the distance of between the estimated position of T_j and either another target $T_{j'}$ in its vicinity, an approaching exit in region R, or other landmarks in the region that might cause occlusion or other difficulties in feature-to-target data association. We define $d^{jj'}$ as

$$d^{jj'} = \min_{j'}\left({}^g\hat{\mathbf{p}}^j - {}^g\hat{\mathbf{p}}^{j'}\right), \tag{5.42}$$

where $T_{j'} \in \{T_1, \ldots, T_{j-1}, T_{j+1}, \ldots, T_{N_T}\}$. Such a choice of g and f, for large κ_g and κ_f, ensures that the maximization of $M_I(\mathbf{a}, T_j)$ for any target is only factored in under the following conditions:

- if all coordinates of all targets are expected to exceed the accuracy specified by $\bar{P}$, or,

- if the distance $d^{jj'}$ of the estimated position of T_j from a neighboring target $T_{j'}$ (static or dynamic) is less than a specified threshold $\bar{d}^j$.

If none of these conditions is satisfied, the second term in Eqn. (5.39) is near zero. Although high priority is given to obtaining high-resolution shots, once all targets are tracked to an accuracy better than $\bar{P}$, if a target is approaching an exit or a cluster of other targets that may hamper data association, it might be imperative to prioritize a high-resolution image capture of that target, even if it leads to sacrificing tracking accuracy.

Bayesian Value   Because the global utility $U_G(\mathbf{a})$ that is actually received is dependent on the random variables ${}^g\mathbf{p}^j(k+1)$ for $j = 1, \ldots, N_T$, through $\mathbf{H}_i^j$ and the FOV, the global utility is a random variable. Therefore, the optimization should be based on the expected value of the global utility function $U_G(\mathbf{a})$ over the distribution of the uncertainty in the estimated position of the target. Hence, we define a Bayesian value function $V(\mathbf{a})$ as:

$$\begin{aligned} V(\mathbf{a}) &= E\left\langle U_G(\mathbf{a}; {}^g\mathbf{p}^j, \ j = 1, \ldots, N_T)\right\rangle \\ &= \int\left(U_{Tr}(\mathbf{a}) + \sum_{j=1}^{N_T}\left(v_j\left(g\left(U_{Tr}\right) + f(d^{jj'})\right) M_I(\mathbf{a}, T_j)\right)\right) p_{\mathbf{p}}\left(\boldsymbol{\zeta}\right) d\boldsymbol{\zeta} . \end{aligned} \tag{5.43}$$

The dummy variable $\boldsymbol{\zeta}$ is used for integration over the ground plane and $p_{\mathbf{p}}$ is the Normal distribution $\mathcal{N}({}^g\hat{\mathbf{p}}^j, \mathbf{P}_{\mathbf{pp}}^{j-})$ of the predicted position of T_j in the global frame at the next imaging instant, where

$\mathbf{P}_{\mathbf{pp}}^{j-}$ represents the position covariance matrix. Note that, $U_{Tr}(\mathbf{a})$ must account for FOV, as discussed after Eqn. (5.21).

The integral represents the area spanned by the FOV of the camera. Inside the integral, the global utility $U_G(\mathbf{a})$ is multiplied by the probability distribution function $p_\mathbf{p}$, where the maximum value for $p_\mathbf{p}$ occurs at the estimated target position $^g\hat{\mathbf{p}}^j$. Thus, integrating over the FOV makes the camera C_i select a settings profile $\mathbf{a}_i$ such that most of the ellipsoid formed by the position covariance matrix $\mathbf{P}_{\mathbf{pp}}^{j-}$ around the position estimate $^g\hat{\mathbf{p}}^j$, is in view, thus eliminating the risk of losing the target. The integration with the probability density function is important in opportunistic sensing since zooming in on a target increases the risk of losing it or some other target.

5.4.2   EXPERIMENTS

We show results in simulation to discuss the performance of the system with the utility functions described in Section 5.3.3, as well as on a real-life distributed camera network surveying an area. First, for a simulated network of cameras, the objective is to highlight the conditions under which cameras in a distributed network collaborate to decide on obtaining high-resolution images of targets in the area, at or close to the desired pose of the target. Next, we extend the approach to a real-life camera network to show *how* and *when* the cameras decide to obtain high-resolution images.

Simulation

At initialization, all the cameras apply the game-theoretic approach detailed in Section 5.3.5 and [Song et al., 2011b] to cover the entire region under surveillance to acquire state estimates of targets already in the region. The target detection module in each camera determines the image plane position of each target in its field-of-view. This information is then passed along to the Extended Kalman-Consensus filter and is processed along with the information from the filters running on neighboring cameras as described in Section 5.1.1. For the simulation and the real life experiment, value for obtaining a high-resolution image would only be added if the tracking performance of the network on all targets met a pre-defined threshold. Also, maximizing the Bayesian Value accounts for the risk of losing the target.

Setup

The area under surveillance was set up as a rectangular region of 20 by 30 m. For the purpose of simulation, we setup a sensor network of $N_C = 4$ calibrated cameras, located on the four corners of the rectangular region, and ran the simulation for $T = 30$ *secs*. All cameras were assumed to have a resolution of 320×240 pixels. Each camera in our setup was assumed to be an independent entity and connected with the entire system.

Optimization

Assume that it is C_i's turn to optimize first. C_i receives camera parameters $\mathbf{a}_{-i}$. It uses its existing parameters $\mathbf{a}_i$, and incoming parameters $\mathbf{a}_{-i}$, to compute Eqn. (5.21) and then optimizes parameters

$\mathbf{a}_i$, with parameters $\mathbf{a}_{-i}$ staying constant. Thus, each camera tries to maximize the global utility by maximizing its own local camera utility, as mentioned in Section 5.3.2.

Results and Discussion

From Figure (5.7) we can see that the cameras cooperate to reduce the tracking covariance at every time step. Once the tracking accuracy is near the predefined threshold, cameras that have the ability to obtain desirable high-resolution images of features may then gain utility for acquiring them. Due to measurement noise, the predicted information and the actual information gained from a measurement may not be equal causing the network to not meet the tracking specification. This causes $g(U_{Tr})$ to drop at time-step t_6 preventing cameras from gaining utility from acquiring high-resolution images of features.

More high-resolution shots are captured at time-steps t_{20} and t_{24}. These images are acquired since the tracking requirements are satisfied and the cameras can obtain better high-resolution images of the features.

Figure (5.8) shows the individual utility functions across simulation time. When the tracking specification is sufficiently satisfied, a sufficiently high value for the weighting function $g(U_{Tr})$ is obtained, which enables the imaging utility $M_I(\mathbf{a})$ to be added to the global utility $U_G(\mathbf{a})$. Thus, in times of opportunity, $M_I(\mathbf{a})$ is added to $U_G(\mathbf{a})$, subject to tracking specification being satisfied, maximizing the global utility.

5.5   CONCLUSIONS

The ability to acquire images based on real-time analysis of the data in the immediate past can enhance the performance of many video analysis systems. In a network of cameras, this also requires coordination between the different cameras since individual decisions at each camera are affected by those of others. In this chapter, we have introduced some ideas that could lead to the development of collaborative sensing strategies in a camera network. The methods have parallels with work in multi-agents systems and cooperative control. Future research in developing the optimization frameworks for various scene understanding tasks should be considered. The integration of multi-agent systems with computer vision has the potential to open up a large number of interesting research problems, especially when considering mobile agents equipped with vision sensors.

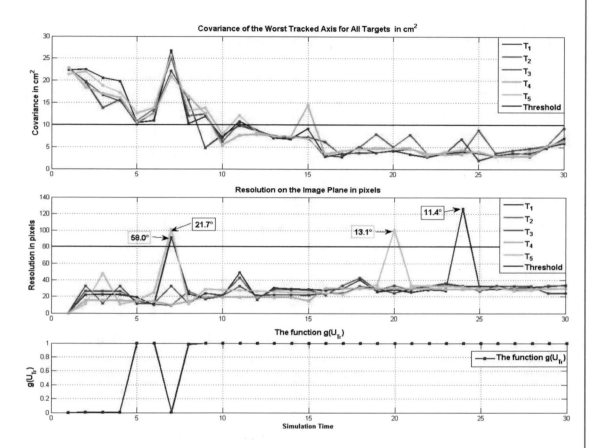

Figure 5.7: Plots for the tracking covariance, image resolution, and the function $g(U_{Tr})$, for $N_T = 5$ targets. As the tracking covariance for all targets approaches the min. covariance threshold of $10cm^2$, for $\kappa_g = 1000$, a non-zero value for imaging utility weight $g(U_{Tr})$ is obtained. Subsequently, at time-step t_7, the resolution, pose and/or distance requirement is met, and high-resolution images of targets T_1 and T_5 are captured at $58.0°$ and $21.7°$ from the desired angle. This causes degradation in tracking performance and the tracking covariance increases. After tracking specifications are met again, more high-resolution images are obtained at time-steps t_{20} and t_{24}, for targets T_1 and T_5, at angular distance of $11.4°$ and $13.1°$. The second set of high-resolution images for the same targets are obtained, due to an improvement over the previous viewing angle.

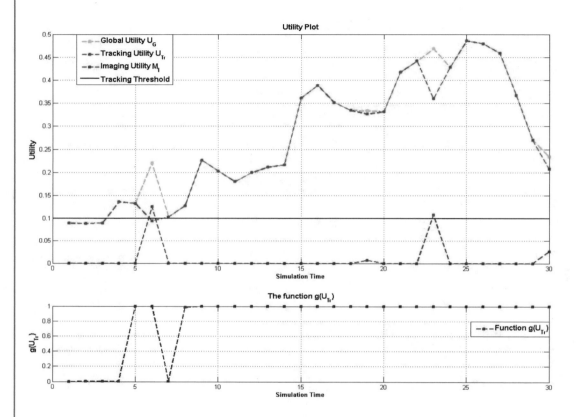

Figure 5.8: Plots of utilities for our simulation. The global utility $U_G(\mathbf{a})$ represents the summation of tracking and imaging utilities. The tracking utility $U_{Tr}(\mathbf{a})$ is a measure of the tracking performance of the least accurately tracked target. As $U_{Tr}(\mathbf{a})$ satisfies tracking threshold $\bar{P}$, a non-zero value for the function $g(U_{Tr})$ is obtained. If pose, resolution and distance requirements for imaging the target are satisfied, then a spike for the imaging utility $M_I(\mathbf{a})$ can be seen. At time-step t_4, the tracking threshold is satisfied, and a non-zero value for $g(U_{Tr})$ is obtained. At time-step t_6 the pose, resolution and/or distance requirement for a target is satisfied and thus a high value for $M_I(\mathbf{a})$ is seen. This results in capture of a high-resolution image of a target, but also leads to degradation in tracking performance, which can be seen in reduction in $U_{Tr}(\mathbf{a})$ at t_6. Another high-resolution image is obtained at t_{23}, leading to degradation in tracking. But, in spite of degradation in $U_{Tr}(\mathbf{a})$, it stays above $\bar{P}$, thus enabling $g(U_{Tr})$ to have a non-zero value.

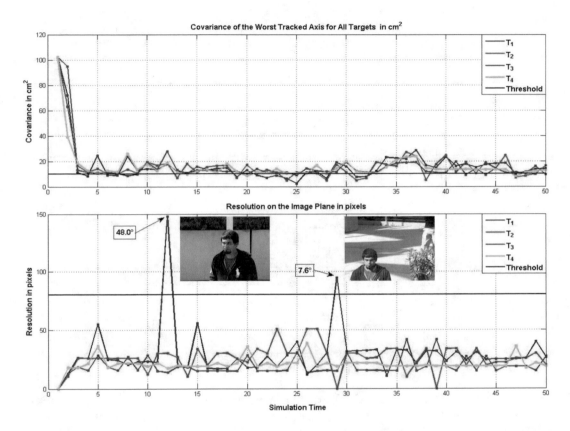

Figure 5.9: Plots for the tracking covariance, image resolution, and the function $g(U_{Tr})$, for $N_T = 4$ targets. As the tracking covariance for all targets approaches the min. covariance threshold of $10cm^2$, for $\kappa_g = 1000$, a non-zero value for imaging utility weight $g(U_{Tr})$ is obtained. Subsequently, at time-step t_{12}, the resolution, pose and/or distance requirement is met, and a high-resolution image of target T_1 is captured at $48.0°$ from the desired angle. This causes degradation in tracking performance and the tracking covariance increases. After tracking specifications are met again, another high-resolution image is obtained at time-step t_{29} for target T_1, at angular distance of $7.6°$. The second high-resolution image for the same target is obtained, due to an improvement over the previous viewing angle.

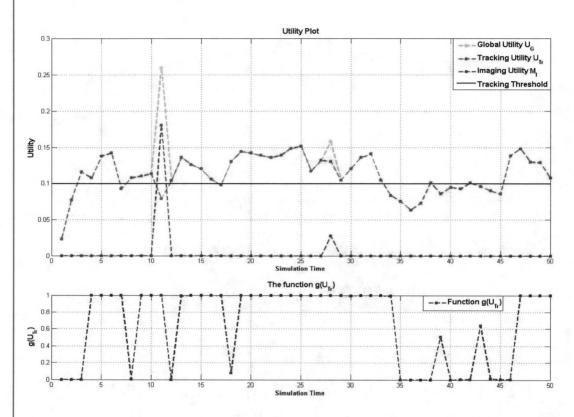

Figure 5.10: Plots of utilities for the real-life experiment performed on a distributed camera network of $N_C = 3$ cameras, to track and image $N_T = 4$ targets. The global utility $U_G(\mathbf{a})$ represents the summation of tracking and imaging utilities. The tracking utility $U_{Tr}(\mathbf{a})$ is a measure of the tracking performance of the least accurately tracked target. As $U_{Tr}(\mathbf{a})$ satisfies tracking threshold $\bar{P}$, a non-zero value for the function $g(U_{Tr})$ is obtained. If pose, resolution and/or distance requirements for imaging the target are satisfied, then a spike for the imaging utility $M_I(\mathbf{a})$ can be seen. At time-step t_7, the tracking threshold is satisfied, and a non-zero value for $g(U_{Tr})$ is obtained. At time-step t_{11} the pose, resolution and/or distance requirement for a target is satisfied and thus a high value for $M_I(\mathbf{a})$ is seen. This results in capture of a high-resolution image of a target, but also leads to degradation in tracking performance, which can be seen in reduction in $U_{Tr}(\mathbf{a})$ at t_{11}. Another high-resolution image is obtained at t_{28}, leading to degradation in tracking. But, in spite of degradation in $U_{Tr}(\mathbf{a})$, it stays above $\bar{P}$, thus enabling $g(U_{Tr})$ to have a non-zero value.

(a) Images at time-step t_{11}

(b) Images at time-step t_{29}

Figure 5.11: Images captured by $N_C = 3$ cameras at time-steps t_{11} and t_{29} of the experiment. The first high-resolution image of a target is acquired at t_{11} by C_3 at angle $48.0°$ from the desired angle. Another high-resolution image of the target is captured by C_2, at t_{29} at an angle $7.6°$ from the desired angle.

CHAPTER 6

Future Research Directions

In the last few chapters, we have discussed the recent developments in the problem of scene understanding from a network of video cameras. We first looked at the problems of wide-area tracking in a network of overlapping and non-overlapping cameras. We presented a few methods that estimate stable, long-term tracks from short tracklets. Thereafter, we considered the problem of distributed processing in camera networks and showed how pose estimation, calibration and tracking can be done in such a setup. Consensus algorithms were presented for all of these tasks. We specifically focused on the problem of distributed tracking and showed how consensus approaches can be used for this purpose. Some of the challenges in object and activity recognition were analyzed and a few solution strategies discussed. Integrated sensing and analysis in camera networks holds promise for optimizing the image acquisition process based on real-time analysis of the data. We discussed existing approaches for achieving this and presented a distributed optimization framework that has parallels to the concept of potential games in game theory. We showed that this approach was also capable of acquiring desirable images whenever the opportunity presented itself.

Future research in camera networks can evolve along two broad themes. The first is based on traditional video analysis problems focused on wide-area scene understanding. This will require addressing issues like handoff between cameras, learning and exploiting traffic patterns, and understanding activities as they evolve over long space-time horizons. Most current work in computer vision is limited to the analysis of short video segments, while wide area scene understanding will require analysis of much longer sequences that evolve continuously in time. Activity recognition work in computer vision has been focused on analysis of single activities and has recently started looking at activities that involve multi-object interactions. However, in most real-life scenarios, multiple activities happen at the same time and a time sequence of activities is usually related (e.g., person exiting a building, entering a car, car starting, and so on). This will require modeling not just single activities but collections of them and building contextual models that represent the relationships between them. Development of such algorithms also calls for the design of efficient system architectures and computational approaches that would be capable of handling the complexity of video analysis algorithms for scene modeling, search and retrieval. Conversely, the computer vision algorithms need to be designed with an awareness of the constraints imposed by real-life networks.

The second major theme for research in camera networks is in developing autonomous systems consisting of fixed and mobile cameras with embedded intelligence capable of video acquisition and analysis over wide areas. This is a highly interdisciplinary area that can bring together researchers in computer vision, control theory, machine learning and various branches of mathematics and statistics. The vision is to develop an intelligent network of mobile agents, each equipped with visual sensors and the capability of analyzing its own data and taking decisions in coordination with other agents. This would enable the agents to maneuver themselves optimally so as to obtain images that can be analyzed with a high degree of reliability. This will require that the system has the ability to jointly optimize camera locations and sensing parameters to satisfy a scene understanding objective. Some initial steps taken in this direction were described in Chapter 5.

This research direction falls within the broad domain of multi-agent systems, which are systems of interacting intelligent agents where each individual is able to sense only a part of the system and communicate with a time-varying set of neighbors. Thus, coordination is central to multi-agent systems. Broadly speaking, coordination refers to an agent being aware of other agents in its environment—be it for resource allocation, task allocation, communication, or movement. When the agents have the capability of moving, coordination must be reflected in both task allocation and motion control, and one primary research topic is the Vehicle Routing Problem (VRP). Equipping these vehicles with cameras would enable tasks in which visual analysis is key, e.g., visual tracking and monitoring, object and event recognition. This leads to the Mobile Camera Networks (MCN) problem, which has some fundamental differences with the VRP problem, as was discussed at the very beginning of the book in Chapter 1. While video analysis will not be the focus of research in this direction, the algorithms would obviously have to be developed with an awareness of the capabilities on the analysis side. Distributed solutions to many of the basic video analysis tasks will be key to these systems. The vision of such multi-agent systems equipped with cameras will also require development of suitable hardware and software platforms that will be able to satisfy the computation and communication requirements. Networking and communication constraints, as well as power resources, will be critical issues in many application domains.

In summary, camera networks is an upcoming area of research with a highly interdisciplinary flavor and a promise for addressing problems in application domains where there is a critical need for such technology, e.g., disaster response, wide area surveillance, assisted living. While many of the building blocks, especially in relation to video analysis, are in place, the network-level solutions, like distributed estimation, resource constraints or integration of sensing and analysis tasks, are very much in their infancy. The area holds a lot of promise for a number of reasons—basic research problems that span multiple disciplines, interdisciplinary research problems that bring together computer science, electrical engineering and mathematics, and technology development that will transition the research into critically necessary application domains.

Bibliography

Alahi, A., Marimon, D., Bierlaire, M., and Kunt, M. (2008). A master-slave approach for object detection and matching with fixed and mobile cameras. In *Intl. Conf. on Image Processing*. DOI: 10.1109/ICIP.2008.4712104 Cited on page(s) 4

Alighanbari, M. and How, J. P. (2006). An unbiased Kalman consensus algorithm. In *American Control Conference*. DOI: 10.1109/ACC.2006.1657263 Cited on page(s) 49

Arslan, G., Marden, J., and Shamma, J. (2007). Autonomous vehicle-target assignment: A game-theoretical formulation. *ASME Journal of Dynamic Systems, Measurement and Control*, 129(5). DOI: 10.1115/1.2766722 Cited on page(s) 76, 77, 79, 86

Arulampalam, M. S., Maskell, S., and Gordon, N. (2002). A tutorial on particle filters for online nonlinear/non-Gaussian Bayesian tracking. *IEEE Trans. on Signal Processing*, 50:174–188. DOI: 10.1109/78.978374 Cited on page(s) 12

Bar-Shalom, Y. and Fortmann, T. (1988). *Tracking and Data Association*. Academic Press. Cited on page(s) 3, 12, 40, 53

Bar-Shalom, Y., Fortmann, T., and Scheffe, M. (1980). Joint probabilistic data assocation for multiple targets in clutter. *Information Sciences and Systmes*. Cited on page(s) 41

Barton-Sweeney, A., Lymberopoulos, D., and Savvides, A. (2006). Sensor localization and camera calibration in distributed camera sensor networks. In *International Conference on Broadband Communications, Networks and Systems*. DOI: 10.1109/BROADNETS.2006.4374301 Cited on page(s) 55

Bertsekas, D. P. and Tsitsiklis, J. (1989). *Parallell and Distributed Computation*. Upper Saddle River, NJ: Prentice-Hall. Cited on page(s) 34

Blake, A. and Yuille, A., editors (1992). *Active Vision*. MIT Press. Cited on page(s) 73

Bland, P., Spurn, P., Towner, M., Bevan, A., Singleton, A., Bottke, W., Greenwood, R., Chesley, S., Shrben, L., Borovika, J., Ceplecha, Z., McClafferty, T., Vaughan, D., Benedix, G., Deacon, G., Howard, K., Franchi, I., and Hough, R. (2009). An anomalous basaltic meteorite from the innermost main belt. *Science*, 325(5947):1525–1527. DOI: 10.1126/science.1174787 Cited on page(s) 8

Blei, D.M., Ng, A.Y., and Jordan, M.I. (2003). Latent dirichlet allocation. *Journal of Machine Learning Research*, 3:993–1022. Cited on page(s) 65

Bullo, F., Frazzoli, E., Pavone, M., Savla, K., and Smith, S. (2011). Dynamic vehicle routing for robotic systems. *Proceedings of the IEEE*, 99(9):1482–1504. DOI: 10.1109/JPROC.2011.2158181 Cited on page(s) 6

Campos-Nanez, E., Garcia, A., and Li, C. (2008). A game-theoretic approach to efficient power management in sensor networks. *Operations Research*, 56(3):552–561. DOI: 10.1287/opre.1070.0435 Cited on page(s) 82

Cham, T. J. and Rehg, J. M. (1999). A multiple hypothesis approach to figure tracking. In *IEEE Conf. on Computer Vision and Pattern Recognition*. DOI: 10.1109/CVPR.1999.784636 Cited on page(s) 67

Chen, L., Cetin, M., and Willsky, A. S. (2005). Distributed data association for multi-target tracking in sensor networks. In *Int'l Conf. Information Fusion*, pages 9–16, Philadelphia, PA, USA. DOI: 10.1109/CDC.2008.4739066 Cited on page(s) 53, 54

Cheng, Z., Devarajan, D., and Radke, R. (2007). Determining vision graphs for distributed camera networks using feature digests. *EURASIP Journal on Advances in Signal Processing: Special Issue on Visual Sensor Networks*. DOI: 10.1155/2007/57034 Cited on page(s) 2

Christoudias, C., Urtasun, R., and Darrell, T. (2008). Unsupervised feature selection via distributed coding for multi-view object recognition. In *IEEE Conf. on Computer Vision and Pattern Recognition*. DOI: 10.1109/CVPR.2008.4587615 Cited on page(s) 60

Comaniciu, D., Ramesh, V., and Meer, P. (2003). Kernel-based object tracking. *IEEE Trans. on Pattern Analysis and Machine Intelligence*. DOI: 10.1109/TPAMI.2003.1195991 Cited on page(s) 21

Cook, D. and Das, S. (2005). *Smart Environments: Technology, Protocols and Applications*. Wiley-Interscience. Cited on page(s) 8

Davis, J. W. (2011). Camera Control and Geo-Registration for Video. In Bhanu, B., Ravishankar, C., Roy-Chowdhury, A. K., Aghajan, H., and Terzopoulos, D., editors, *Distributed Video Sensor Networks*. Springer. Cited on page(s) 5

DeGroot, M. (1974). Reaching a consensus. *Journal of the American Statistical Association*, 69(345):118–121. DOI: 10.2307/2285509 Cited on page(s) 34

Denina, G., Bhanu, B., Nguyen, H., Ding, C., Kamal, A., Ravishankar, C., Roy-Chowdhury, A. K., Ivers, A., , and Varda, B. (2011). VideoWeb Dataset for Multi-camera Activities and Non-verbal Communication. In Bhanu, B., Ravishankar, C., Roy-Chowdhury, A., Aghajan, H., and Terzopoulos, D., editors, *Distributed Video Sensor Networks*. Springer. Cited on page(s) 8, 24

Devarajan, D., Cheng, Z., and Radke, R. J. (2008a). Calibrating distributed camera networks. *Proceedings of the IEEE Special Issure on Distributed Smart Cameras*, 96(10):1625–1639. DOI: 10.1109/JPROC.2008.928759 Cited on page(s) 4

Devarajan, D., Cheng, Z., and Radke, R. J. (2008b). Calibrating distributed camera networks. *Proceedings of the IEEE*, 96(10):1625–1639. DOI: 10.1109/JPROC.2008.928759 Cited on page(s) 55

Devarajan, D. and Radke, R. J. (2007). Calibrating distributed camera networks using belief propagation. *EURASIP Journal of Applied Signal Processing*, 2007(1):1–10. DOI: 10.1155/2007/60696 Cited on page(s) 54, 55

Dixon, M., Jacobs, N., and Pless, R. (2009). An efficient system for vehicle tracking in multi-camera networks. In *IEEE/ACM Intl. Conf. on Distributed Smart Cameras*, pages 1–8, Como, Italy. DOI: 10.1109/ICDSC.2009.5289383 Cited on page(s) 53

Doretto, G., Sebastian, T., Tu, P., and Rittscher, J. (2011). Appearance-based person reidentification in camera networks: Problem overview and current approaches. *Journal of Ambient Intelligence and Humanized Computing*, 2:127–151. DOI: 10.1007/s12652-010-0034-y Cited on page(s) 17, 24, 25, 26, 27

Doucet, A., Freitas, N. de, and Gordon, N. (2001). *Sequential Monte Carlo Methods in Practice*. Springer. Cited on page(s) 67

Du, W. and Piater, J. (2007). Multi-camera people tracking by collaborative particle filters and principal axis-based integration. In *Asian Conf. on Computer Vision*. DOI: 10.1007/978-3-540-76386-4_34 Cited on page(s) 17

Duda, R., Hart, P., and Stork, D. (2001). *Pattern Classification*. Wiley-Interscience. Cited on page(s) 22

Egerstedt, M. and Hu, X. (2001). Formation control with virtual leaders and reduced communications. *IEEE Trans. Robotics and Automation*, 17(6):947–951. DOI: 10.1109/70.976029 Cited on page(s) 34

Elhamifar, E. and Vidal, R. (2009). Distributed calibration of camera sensor networks. In *IEEE/ACM Intl. Conf. on Distributed Smart Cameras*, pages 1–8, Como, Italy. DOI: 10.1109/ICDSC.2009.5289397 Cited on page(s) 54, 55

Erdem, U. and Sclaroff, S. (2006). Automated camera layout to satisfy task-specific and floor plan-specific coverage requirements. *Computer Vision Image Understanding*, 103(3):156–169. DOI: 10.1016/j.cviu.2006.06.005 Cited on page(s) 5, 77, 88

Ermis, E., Saligrama, V., Jodoin, P., and Konrad, J. (2008). Abnormal behavior detection and behavior matching for networked cameras. In *IEEE/ACM Intl. Conf. on Distributed Smart Cameras*. DOI: 10.1109/ICDSC.2008.4635728 Cited on page(s) 4

Ermis, E. B., Clarot, P., Jodoin, P. M., and Saligrama, V. (2010). Activity based matching in distributed camera networks. *IEEE Trans. on Image Processing*, 19(10):2564–2579. DOI: 10.1109/TIP.2010.2052823 Cited on page(s) 53

Farenzena, M., Bazzani, L., Perina, A., Cristani, M., and Murino, V. (2010). Person re-identification by symmetry-driven accumulation of local features. In *IEEE Conf. on Computer Vision and Pattern Recognition*. DOI: 10.1109/CVPR.2010.5539926 Cited on page(s) 17

Farrell, R. and Davis, L. S. (2008). Decentralized discovery of camera network topology. In *IEEE/ACM Intl. Conf. on Distributed Smart Cameras*. DOI: 10.1109/ICDSC.2008.4635696 Cited on page(s) 2

Farrell, R., Doermann, D., and Davis, L. S. (2007). Learning higher-order transition models in medium-scale camera networks. In *IEEE Workshop on Omnidirectional Vision*. DOI: 10.1109/ICCV.2007.4409203 Cited on page(s) 2

Fax, J. A. (2001). *Optimal and Cooperative Control of Vehicle Formations*. PhD thesis, California Institute of Technology, Pasadena, CA. Cited on page(s) 34

Ferrari, V., Tuytelaars, T., and Van Gool, L. (2004). Integrating multiple model views for object recognition. In *IEEE Conf. on Computer Vision and Pattern Recognition*. DOI: 10.1109/CVPR.2004.1315151 Cited on page(s) 60

Fortmann, T., Bar-Shalom, Y., and Scheffe, M. (1983). Sonar tracking of multiple targets using joint probabilistic data association. *IEEE Journal of Oceanic Engineering*, 8(3). DOI: 10.1109/JOE.1983.1145560 Cited on page(s) 41

Fudenberg, D. and Levine, D. K. (1998). *The Theory of Learning in Games*. Series on Economic Learning and Social Evolution. MIT Press, Cambridge, MA. Cited on page(s) 5, 76, 77, 79

Gheissari, N., Sebastian, T., and Hartley, R. (2006). Person re-identification using spatiotemporal appearance. In *IEEE Conf. on Computer Vision and Pattern Recognition*. DOI: 10.1109/CVPR.2006.223 Cited on page(s) 17

Gilbert, A. and Bowden, R. (2008). Incremental, scalable tracking of objects inter camera. *Computer Vision and Image Understanding*, 111(1):43–58. DOI: 10.1016/j.cviu.2007.06.005 Cited on page(s) 28, 29

Gray, D. and Tao, H. (2008). Viewpoint invariant pedestrian recognition with an ensemble of localized features. In *Euro. Conf. on Computer Vision*. DOI: 10.1007/978-3-540-88682-2_21 Cited on page(s) 16

Hartley, R. (1994). Self-calibration from multiple views with a rotating camera. In *Euro. Conf. on Computer Vision*. DOI: 10.1007/3-540-57956-7_52 Cited on page(s) 54

Hatano, Y. and Mesbahi, M. (2005). Agreement over random networks. *IEEE Trans. Automatic Control*, 50(11):1867–1872. DOI: 10.1109/TAC.2005.858670 Cited on page(s) 34

Hofmann, T. (1999). Probabilistic latent semantic analysis. In *Conference on Uncertainty in Artificial Intelligence*. Cited on page(s) 65

Hoiem, D., Efros, A., and Hebert, M. (2005). Geometric context from a single image. In *IEEE Intl. Conf. on Computer Vision*. DOI: 10.1109/ICCV.2005.107 Cited on page(s) 12

Hotelling, H. (1936). Relations between two sets of variates. *Biometrika*, 28(3/4):321–377. DOI: 10.2307/2333955 Cited on page(s) 63

Huang, T. and Russel, S. (1997). Object identification in a Bayesian context. In *Proceeding of IJCAI*. Cited on page(s) 3, 16

Hue, C., Cadre, J. L., and Prez, P. (2002). Sequential Monte Carlo methods for multiple target tracking and data fusion. *IEEE Trans. on Signal Processing*, 50(2):309–325. DOI: 10.1109/78.978386 Cited on page(s) 11

Isard, M. and Blake, A. (1998). Condensation - conditional density propagation for visual tracking. *International Journal of Computer Vision*. DOI: 10.1023/A:1008078328650 Cited on page(s) 11, 21

J. Aloimonos, I. Weiss, A. Bandopadhyay (1988). Active vision. *international Journal of Computer Vision*, pages 333–356. DOI: 10.1007/BF00133571 Cited on page(s) 73

Jadbabaie, A., Lin, J., and Morse, A. S. (2003). Coordination of groups of mobile autonomous agents using nearest neighbor rules. *IEEE Trans. Automatic Control*, 48(6):988–1001. DOI: 10.1109/TAC.2003.812781 Cited on page(s) 4, 34

Jannotti, J. and Mao, J. (2006). Distributed calibration of smart cameras. In *International Workshop on Distributed Smart Cameras*. Cited on page(s) 55

Javed, O., Khan, S., Rasheed, Z., and Shah, M. (2000). Camera handoff: Tracking in multiple uncalibrated stationary cameras. In *IEEE Workshop on Human Motion*, pages 113–118, Los Alamitos, CA, USA. DOI: 10.1109/HUMO.2000.897380 Cited on page(s) 4, 53

Javed, O., Rasheed, Z., Shafique, K., and Shah, M. (2003). Tracking across multiple cameras with disjoint views. In *IEEE Intl. Conf. on Computer Vision*. DOI: 10.1109/ICCV.2003.1238451 Cited on page(s) 2, 3, 14, 16, 21, 42

Jiang, H., Fels, S., and Little, J. (2007). A linear programming approach for multiple object tracking. In *IEEE Conf. on Computer Vision and Pattern Recognition*. DOI: 10.1109/CVPR.2007.383180 Cited on page(s) 3, 14, 53

Kalman, R. (1960). A new approach to linear filtering and prediction problems. *Transaction of the ASME - Journal of Basic Engineering*, 82(Series D):35–45. DOI: 10.1115/1.3662552 Cited on page(s) 11

Kamal, A., Ding, C., Song, B., Farrell, J. A., and Roy-Chowdhury, A. K. (2011). A generalized Kalman consensus filter for wide-area video networks. In *50th IEEE Conf. on Decision and Control and Euro. Control Conference*, Orlando, FL, USA. Cited on page(s) 48

Kang, J., Cohen, I., and Medioni, G. (2004). Continuous tracking within and across camera streams. In *IEEE Conf. on Computer Vision and Pattern Recognition*. DOI: 10.1109/CVPR.2003.1211363 Cited on page(s) 3, 16

Kettnaker, V. and Zabih, R. (1999). Bayesian multi-camera surveillance. In *IEEE Conf. on Computer Vision and Pattern Recognition*. DOI: 10.1109/CVPR.1999.784638 Cited on page(s) 3, 16

Khan, S. and Shah, M. (2003). Consistent labeling of tracked objects in multiple cameras with overlapping fields of view. *IEEE Trans. on Pattern Analysis and Machine Intelligence*, 25(10):1355–1360. DOI: 10.1109/TPAMI.2003.1233912 Cited on page(s) 17, 30

Khan, S.M. and Shah, M. (2006). A multiview approach to tracking people in crowded scenes using a planar homography constraint. In *Euro. Conf. on Computer Vision*. Cited on page(s) 17

Kim, K. and Davis, L. S. (2006). Multi-camera tracking and segmentation of occluded people on ground plane using search-guided particle filtering. In *Euro. Conf. on Computer Vision*. DOI: 10.1007/11744078_8 Cited on page(s) 35

Kuhn, Harold W. (1955). The hungarian method for the assignment problem. *Naval Research Logistics Quarterly*, 2:83–97. DOI: 10.1002/nav.3800020109 Cited on page(s) 21, 42, 53

Kuo, C. H., Huang, C., and Nevatia, R. (2010). Inter-camera association of multi-target tracks by on-line learned appearance affinity models. In *Euro. Conf. on Computer Vision*. Cited on page(s) 16, 17, 18, 19, 20

Kurillo, G., Li, Z., and Bajcsy, R. (2008). Wide-area external multi-camera calibration using vision graphs and virtual calibration object. In *IEEE/ACM Intl. Conf. on Distributed Smart Cameras*. DOI: 10.1109/ICDSC.2008.4635695 Cited on page(s) 55

Leibe, B., Schindler, K., and Gool, L. V. (2007). Coupled detection and trajectory estimation for multi-object tracking. In *IEEE Intl. Conf. on Computer Vision*. DOI: 10.1109/ICCV.2007.4408936 Cited on page(s) 3, 14

Leoputra, W., Tan, T., and Lim, F. L. (2006). Non-overlapping distributed tracking using particle filter. In *Intl. Conf. on Pattern Recognition*. DOI: 10.1109/ICPR.2006.862 Cited on page(s) 3, 16

Li, N. and Marden, J. (2011). Designing games for distributed optimization. In *IEEE Conf. on Decision and Control*, Florida, USA. Cited on page(s) 82

Liao, L., Fox, D., and Kautz, H. (2005). Location-based activity recognition using relational markov networks. In *Proc. of the International Joint Conference on Artificial Intelligence*. Cited on page(s) 67

Liao, T. W. (2005). Clustering of time series data - a survey. *Pattern Recognition*, 38(11):1857–1874. DOI: 10.1016/j.patcog.2005.01.025 Cited on page(s) 62

Lin, Z., Brouke, M., and Francis, B. (2004). Local control strategies for groups of mobile autonomous agents. *IEEE-Trans. Automatic Control*, 49(4):622–629. DOI: 10.1109/TAC.2004.825639 Cited on page(s) 34

Lowe, D. (1999). Object recognition from local scale-invariant features. In *IEEE Intl. Conf. on Computer Vision*. DOI: 10.1109/ICCV.1999.790410 Cited on page(s) 60

Loy, C., Xiang, T., and Gong, S. (2009). Multi-camera activity correlation analysis. In *IEEE Conf. on Computer Vision and Pattern Recognition*. DOI: 10.1109/CVPR.2009.5206827 Cited on page(s) 17

Loy, C. C., Xiang, T., and Gong, S. (2010). Time-delayed correlation analysis for multi-camera activity understanding. *International Journal of Computer Vision*, 90(1):106–129. DOI: 10.1007/s11263-010-0347-5 Cited on page(s) 28, 61, 63

Lynch, Nancy (1996). *Distributed Algorithms*. Morgan Kaufmann Publishers, San Mateo, CA. Cited on page(s) 34

Mandel, Z., Shimshoni, I., and Keren, D. (2007). Multicamera topology recovery from coherent motion. In *IEEE/ACM Intl. Conf. on Distributed Smart Cameras*. DOI: 10.1109/ICDSC.2007.4357530 Cited on page(s) 2

Markis, D., Ellis, T., and Black, J. (2004). Bridging the gap between cameras. In *IEEE Conf. on Computer Vision and Pattern Recognition*. DOI: 10.1109/CVPR.2004.1315165 Cited on page(s) 2, 4, 15, 28, 53

Maybank, S. and Faugeras, O. D. (1992). A theory of selfcalibration of a moving camera. *International Journal of Computer Vision*, 8(2):123–151. DOI: 10.1007/BF00127171 Cited on page(s) 54

Medeiros, H., Park, J., and Kak, A. (2008). Distributed object tracking using a cluster-based Kalman filter in wireless camera networks. *IEEE Journal of Selected Topics in Signal Processing*, 2(4):448–463. DOI: 10.1109/JSTSP.2008.2001310 Cited on page(s) 4, 36, 46

Mehyar, M., Spanos, D., Pongsjapan, J., Low, S., and Murray, R. M. (2005). Distributed averaging on asynchronous communication networks. In *IEEE Conf. on Decision and Control and Euro. Control Conference*, pages 7446–7451. DOI: 10.1109/TNET.2007.893226 Cited on page(s) 34

Mesbahi, M. (2005). On state-dependent dynamic graphs and their controllability properties. *IEEE Trans. Automatic Control*, 50(3):387–392. DOI: 10.1109/TAC.2005.843858 Cited on page(s) 34

Micheloni, C., Rinner, B., and Foresti, G. L. (2010). Video analysis in pan-tilt-zoom camera networks. *IEEE Signal Processing Magazine*, 27(5):78–90. DOI: 10.1109/MSP.2010.937333 Cited on page(s) 77

Mikolajczyk, K. and Schmid, C. (2005). A performance evaluation of local descriptors. *IEEE Trans. on Pattern Analysis and Machine Intelligence*, 27:11615–1630. DOI: 10.1109/TPAMI.2005.188 Cited on page(s) 27

Mittal, A. and Davis, L. S. (2008). A general method for sensor planning in multi-sensor systems: Extension to random occlusion. *International Journal of Computer Vision*, 76:31–52. DOI: 10.1007/s11263-007-0057-9 Cited on page(s) 5, 77, 78

Monderer, D. and Shapley, L. S. (1996). Potential games. *Games and Economic Behavior*, 14(1). DOI: 10.1006/game.1996.0044 Cited on page(s) 81, 86

Morye, A. A., Ding, C., Song, B., Roy-Chowdhury, A. K., and Farrell, J. A. (2011). Optimized imaging and target tracking within a distributed camera network. In *American Control Conference*. Cited on page(s) 75, 76

Nayak, N., Sethi, R., Song, B., and Roy-Chowdhury, A. K. (2011). Motion pattern analysis for modeling and recognition of complex human activities. In Moeslund, Th.B., Hilton, A., Krüger, V., and Sigal, L., editors, *Visual Analysis of Humans*. Springer. Cited on page(s) 59

Niu, C. and Grimson, E. (2006). Recovering non-overlapping network topology using far-field vehicle tracking. In *Intl. Conf. on Pattern Recognition*. DOI: 10.1109/ICPR.2006.985 Cited on page(s) 2, 15

North, B., Blake, A., Isard, M., and Rittscher, J. (2000). Learning and classification of complex dynamics. *IEEE Trans. on Pattern Analysis and Machine Intelligence*, 22(9):1016–1034. DOI: 10.1109/34.877523 Cited on page(s) 67

Ocean, Michael, Bestavros, Azer, and Kfoury, Assaf (2006). snBench: Programming and virtualization framework for distributed multitasking sensor networks. In *Proceedings of the 2nd international conference on Virtual execution environments (VEE 2006)*, pages 89 – 99, New York, NY, USA. ACM Press. DOI: 10.1145/1134760.1134774 Cited on page(s) 8

Olfati-Saber, R. (2005). Ultrafast consensus in small-world networks. *American Control Conference*, pages 2371–2378. DOI: 10.1109/ACC.2005.1470321 Cited on page(s) 34

Olfati-Saber, R. (2006). Flocking for multi-agent dynamic systems: Algorithms and theory. *IEEE Trans. Automatic Control*, 51(3):401–420. DOI: 10.1109/TAC.2005.864190 Cited on page(s) 34

Olfati-Saber, R. (2007). Distributed Kalman filtering for sensor networks. In *IEEE Conf. on Decision and Control*, pages 5492–5498, New Orleans, LA, USA. DOI: 10.1109/CDC.2007.4434303 Cited on page(s) 34, 36, 46, 69

Olfati-Saber, R. (2009). Kalman-consensus filter: Optimality, stability, and performance. In *IEEE Conf. on Decision and Control and Chinese Control Conference*, pages 7036–7042, Shanghai, China. DOI: 10.1109/CDC.2009.5399678 Cited on page(s) 36, 49

Olfati-Saber, R., Fax, J. A., and Murray, R. M. (2007). Consensus and cooperation in networked multi-agent systems. *Proceedings of the IEEE*, 95(1):215–233. DOI: 10.1109/JPROC.2006.887293 Cited on page(s) 4, 34, 50

Olfati-Saber, R. and Murray, R. M. (2004). Consensus problems in networks of agents with switching topology and time-delays. *IEEE Trans. Automatic Control*, 49(9):1520–1533. DOI: 10.1109/TAC.2004.834113 Cited on page(s) 4, 34

Olfati-Saber, R. and Sandell, N. F. (2008). Distributed tracking in sensor networks with limited sensing range. In *American Control Conference*, pages 3157 – 3162, Seattle, WA, USA. DOI: 10.1109/ACC.2008.4586978 Cited on page(s) 36, 38, 40, 75

Perera, A., Srinivas, C., Hoogs, A., Brooksby, G., and Hu, W. (2006). Multi-object tracking through simultaneous long occlusions and split-merge conditions. In *IEEE Conf. on Computer Vision and Pattern Recognition*. DOI: 10.1109/CVPR.2006.195 Cited on page(s) 3, 14

Piciarelli, C., Micheloni, C., and Foresti, G.L. (2009). PTZ camera network reconfiguration. In *IEEE/ACM Intl. Conf. on Distributed Smart Cameras*, pages 1–8, Como, Italy. DOI: 10.1109/ICDSC.2009.5289419 Cited on page(s) 5, 77, 78

Pollefeys, M., Koch, R., and Gool, L. Van (1999). Self-calibration and metric reconstruction in spite of varying and unknown intrinsic camera parameters. *International Journal of Computer Vision*, 32(1):7–25. DOI: 10.1023/A:1008109111715 Cited on page(s) 54

Preciado, V. M. and Verghese, G. C. (2005). Synchronization in generalized Erdös-Rényi networks of nonlinear oscillators. In *IEEE Conf. on Decision and Control and Euro. Control Conference*. Cited on page(s) 34

Prosser, B., Zheng, W., Gong, S., and Xiang, T. (2010). Person re-identification by support vector ranking. In *British Machine Vision Conference*. DOI: 10.5244/C.24.21 Cited on page(s) 16

Quintero, S., Papi, F., Klein, D., Chisci, L., and Hespanha, J. (2010). Optimal uav coordination for target tracking using dynamic programming. In *IEEE Conf. on Decision and Control*. DOI: 10.1109/CDC.2010.5717933 Cited on page(s) 7

Qureshi, F. Z. and Terzopoulos, D. (2007).   Surveillance in virtual reality: System design and multi-camera control.   In *IEEE Conf. on Computer Vision and Pattern Recognition*. DOI: 10.1109/CVPR.2007.383071 Cited on page(s) 4, 36

Qureshi, F. Z. and Terzopoulos, D. (2009). Planning ahead for PTZ camera assignment and handoff. In *IEEE/ACM Intl. Conf. on Distributed Smart Cameras*, pages 1–8, Como, Italy. DOI: 10.1109/ICDSC.2009.5289420 Cited on page(s) 5, 77, 78

Rahimi, A. and Darrell, T. (2004). Simultaneous calibration and tracking with a network of non-overlapping sensors. In *IEEE Conf. on Computer Vision and Pattern Recognition*. DOI: 10.1109/CVPR.2004.1315031 Cited on page(s) 3, 4, 16, 53

Reid, D. (1979).   An algorithm for tracking multiple targets.   *IEEE Trans. Automatic Control*, 24(6):843–854. DOI: 10.1109/TAC.1979.1102177 Cited on page(s) 3, 12, 53

Ren, W., Beard, A. W., and Kingston, D. B. (2005). Multi-agent Kalman consensus with relative uncertainty. In *American Control Conference*. DOI: 10.1109/ACC.2005.1470240 Cited on page(s) 49

Ren, W. and Beard, R. W. (2005).   Consensus seeking in multi-agent systems under dynamically changing interaction topologies.   *IEEE Trans. Automatic Control*, 50(5):655–661. DOI: 10.1109/TAC.2005.846556 Cited on page(s) 34

Rittscher, J. and Black, A. (1999). Classification of human body motion. In *IEEE Intl. Conf. on Computer Vision*. DOI: 10.1109/ICCV.1999.791284 Cited on page(s) 67

Rosencrantz, M., Gordon, G., and Thrun, S. (2003). Decentralized sensor fusion with distributed particle filters. In *Conf. Uncertainty in AI*. Cited on page(s) 35

Sandell, N. F. and Olfati-Saber, R. (2008). Distributed data association for multi-target tracking in sensor networks. In *IEEE Conference on Decision and Control*, pages 1085 –1090. DOI: 10.1109/CDC.2008.4739066 Cited on page(s) 42, 53

Sankaranarayanan, A.C., Veeraraghavan, A., and Chellappa, R. (2008). Object detection, tracking and recognition for multiple smart cameras. *Proceedings of the IEEE Special Issure on Distributed Smart Cameras*, 96(10):1606–1624. DOI: 10.1109/JPROC.2008.928758 Cited on page(s) 4

Scutari, G., Palomar, D. P., and Pang, J. (2009). Flexible design of conitive radio wireless systems: From game theory to variational inequality theory. *IEEE Signal Processing Magazine*, 26(5):107–123. DOI: 10.1109/MSP.2009.933446 Cited on page(s) 82

Shafique, K. and Shah, M. (2005). A non-iterative greedy algorithm for multi-frame point correspondence. *IEEE Trans. on Pattern Analysis and Machine Intelligence*. DOI: 10.1109/TPAMI.2005.1 Cited on page(s) 14

Song, B., Ding, C., Kamal, A., Farrell, J. A., and Roy-Chowdhury, A. K. (2011a). Distributed camera networks: Integrated sensing and analysis for wide area scene understanding. *IEEE Signal Processing Magazine*, 3:20–31. Cited on page(s) 48, 92, 93

Song, B., Ding, C., Roy-Chowdhury, A., and Farrell, J. A. (2011b). Persistent observation of dynamic scenes in an active camera network. In Bhanu, B., Ravishankar, C., Roy-Chowdhury, A. K., Aghajan, H., and Terzopoulos, D., editors, *Distributed Video Sensor Networks*. Springer. Cited on page(s) 91, 95

Song, B., Jeng, T., Staudt, E., and Roy-Chowdhury, A. K. (2010a). A stochastic graph evolution framework for robust multi-target tracking. In *Euro. Conf. on Computer Vision*. DOI: 10.1007/978-3-642-15549-9_44 Cited on page(s) 17, 19, 21, 22

Song, B., Kamal, A., Soto, C., Ding, C., Farrell, J. A., and Roy-Chowdhury, A. K. (2010b). Tracking and activity recognition through consensus in distributed camera network. *IEEE Trans. on Image Processing*, 19(10):2564–2579. DOI: 10.1109/TIP.2010.2052823 Cited on page(s) 4, 37, 45, 47, 48, 67, 69, 71, 72, 84

Song, B. and Roy-Chowdhury, A. (2007). Stochastic adaptive tracking in a camera network. In *IEEE Intl. Conf. on Computer Vision*. DOI: 10.1109/ICCV.2007.4408937 Cited on page(s) 3, 4, 74

Song, B. and Roy-Chowdhury, A. (2008). Robust tracking in a camera network: A multi-objective optimization framework. *IEEE Journal on Selected Topics in Signal Processing: Special Issue on Distributed Processing in Vision Networks*. DOI: 10.1109/JSTSP.2008.925992 Cited on page(s) 3, 15, 17, 19, 21, 24

Song, B., Sethi, R., and Roy-Chowdhury, A. (2011c). Wide area tracking in single and multiple views. In Moeslund, T., Hilton, A., Krüger, V., and Sigal, L., editors, *Visual Analysis of Humans: Looking at People*. Springer. Cited on page(s) 24

Soto, C., Song, B., and Roy-Chowdhury, A. K. (2009). Distributed multi-target tracking in a self-configuring camera network. In *IEEE Conf. on Computer Vision and Pattern Recognition*. DOI: 10.1109/CVPR.2009.5206773 Cited on page(s) 5, 44, 77, 78, 88

Stancil, B., Zhang, C., and Chen, T. (2008). Active multicamera networks: From rendering to surveillance. *IEEE Journal on Selected Topics in Signal Processing Special Issue on Distributed Processing in Vision Networks*. DOI: 10.1109/JSTSP.2008.2001305 Cited on page(s) 4

Stauffer, C. and Grimson, W. E. L. (1998). Adaptive background mixture models for real-time tracking. In *IEEE Conf. on Computer Vision and Pattern Recognition*. DOI: 10.1109/CVPR.1999.784637 Cited on page(s) 12

Sturges, J. and Whitfield, T.W.A. (1995). Locating basic colour in the munsell space. *Color Research and Application*, 20(6):364–376. DOI: 10.1002/col.5080200605 Cited on page(s) 28

Swain, M. and Ballard, D. (1991). Color indexing. *International Journal of Computer Vision*, 7(1):11–32. DOI: 10.1007/BF00130487 Cited on page(s) 26

Taj, M. and Cavaliaro, A. (2011). Distributed and decentralized multicamera tracking. *IEEE Signal Processing Magazine*, 3:46–58. DOI: 10.1109/MSP.2011.940281 Cited on page(s) 35

Terzopoulos, D. (2003). Perceptive agents and systems in virtual reality. In *Proc. ACM Symposium on Virtual Reality Software and Technology*, Osaka, Japan. DOI: 10.1145/1008653.1008655 Cited on page(s) 7

Terzopoulos, D. and Qureshi, F. Z. (2011). Virtual vision: Virtual reality subserving computer vision research for camera sensor networks. In Bhanu, B., Ravishankar, C., Roy-Chowdhury, A., Aghajan, H., and Terzopoulos, D., editors, *Distributed Video Sensor Networks*. Springer. Cited on page(s) 7

Thomas, A., Ferrar, V., Leibe, B., Tuytelaars, T., Schiel, B., and Van Gool, L. (2006). Towards multi-view object class detection. In *IEEE Conf. on Computer Vision and Pattern Recognition*. DOI: 10.1109/CVPR.2006.311 Cited on page(s) 60

Tieu, K., Dalley, G., and Grimson, W. E. L. (2005). Inference of non-overlapping camera network topology by measuring statistical dependence. In *IEEE Intl. Conf. on Computer Vision*. DOI: 10.1109/ICCV.2005.122 Cited on page(s) 2, 4, 28

Triggs, B. (1997). Autocalibration and the absolute quadric. In *IEEE Conf. on Computer Vision and Pattern Recognition*. DOI: 10.1109/CVPR.1997.609388 Cited on page(s) 54

Tron, R., Vidal, R., and Terzis., A. (2008). Distributed pose averaging in camera sensor networks via consensus on SE(3). In *IEEE/ACM Intl. Conf. on Distributed Smart Cameras*. DOI: 10.1109/ICDSC.2008.4635701 Cited on page(s) 4, 56

Tsai, R. Y. (1986). An efficient and accurate camera calibration technique for 3d machine vision. In *IEEE Conf. on Computer Vision and Pattern Recognition*. Cited on page(s) 54

Tsitsiklis, J. N., Bertsekas, D. P., and Athans, M. (1986). Distributed asynchronous deterministic and stochastic gradient optimization algorithms. *IEEE Trans. Automatic Control*, 31(9):803–812. DOI: 10.1109/TAC.1986.1104412 Cited on page(s) 34

Turaga, P., Chellappa, R., Subrahmanian, V. S., and Udrea, O. (2008). Machine recognition of human activities: A survey. *IEEE Trans. on Circuits and Systems for Video Technology*. DOI: 10.1109/TCSVT.2008.2005594 Cited on page(s) 59

Wang, X., Tieu, K., and Grimson, E. L. (2010a). Correspondence-free activity analysis and scene modeling in multiple camera views. *IEEE Trans. on Pattern Analysis and Machine Intelligence*, 32(1):56–71. DOI: 10.1109/TPAMI.2008.241 Cited on page(s) 64, 65, 66

Wang, Y., Huang, K., and Tan, T. (2007). Multi-view gymnastic activity recognition recognith with fused hmm. In *Asian Conf. on Computer Vision*. Cited on page(s) 66

Wang, Y., Velipasalar, S., and Casares, M. (2010b). Cooperative object tracking and composite event detection with wireless embedded smart cameras. *IEEE Trans. on Image Processing*, 19(10):2595–2613. DOI: 10.1109/TIP.2010.2052278 Cited on page(s) 53

Weinland, D., Boyer, E., and Ronfard, R. (2007). Action recognition from arbitrary views using 3d exemplars. In *IEEE Intl. Conf. on Computer Vision*. DOI: 10.1109/ICCV.2007.4408849 Cited on page(s) 66, 69

Welch, G. and Bishop, G. (1995). An introduction to the Kalman filter. Technical report, University of North Carolina at Chapel Hill, Chapel Hill, NC, USA. Cited on page(s) 12

Wolpert, D. and Tumor, K. (2004). A survey of collectives. In Tumer, K. and Wolpert, D., editors, *Collectives and the Design of Complex Systems*. Springer-Verlag, New York, NY. Cited on page(s) 86

Wu, C. and Aghajan, H. (2008). Real-time human pose estimation: A case study in algorithm design for smart camera networks. *Proceedings of the IEEE Special Issure on Distributed Smart Cameras*, 96(10):1715–1732. DOI: 10.1109/JPROC.2008.928766 Cited on page(s) 4

Xu, Jiejun, Ni, Zefeng, Leo, Carter De, Kuo, Thomas, , and Manjunath, B.S. (2010). Spatial-temporal understanding of urban scenes through large camera network. In *ACM International Conference on Multimedia (2010), Workshop on "Multimodal Pervasive Video Analysis"*. DOI: 10.1145/1878039.1878046 Cited on page(s) 8

Yang, A., Maji, S., Christoudas, M., Darrell, T., Malik, J., and Sastry, S. (2009). Multiple-view object recognition in band-limited distributed camera networks. In *IEEE/ACM Intl. Conf. on Distributed Smart Cameras*. DOI: 10.1109/ICDSC.2009.5289410 Cited on page(s) 60, 61

Yeo, C., Ahammad, P., and Ramchandran, K. (2008). Rate-efficient visual correspondences using random projections. In *Intl. Conf. on Image Processing*. IEEE. DOI: 10.1109/ICIP.2008.4711730 Cited on page(s) 60

Young, H. P. (1998). *Individual Strategy and Social Structure: An Evolutionary Theory of Institutions*. Princeton University Press. Cited on page(s) 82, 86

Yu, Q., Medioni, G., and Cohen, I. (2007). Multiple target tracking using spatio-temporal Markov chain Monte Carlo data association. In *IEEE Conf. on Computer Vision and Pattern Recognition*. DOI: 10.1109/CVPR.2007.382991 Cited on page(s) 3, 14

Zelnik-Manor, L. and Perona, P. (2004). Self-tuning spectral clustering. In *Advances in Neural Information Processing Systems (NIPS)*. Cited on page(s) 63

Zhang, F. and Leonard, N. (2010). Cooperative filters and control for cooperative exploration. *IEEE Trans. Automatic Control*, 55(3):650–663. DOI: 10.1109/TAC.2009.2039240 Cited on page(s) 6

Zhang, L., Li, Y., and Nevatia, R. (2008). Global data association for multi-object tracking using network flows. In *IEEE Conf. on Computer Vision and Pattern Recognition*. DOI: 10.1109/CVPR.2008.4587584 Cited on page(s) 53

Zhang, Z. (2000). A flexible new technique for camera calibration. *IEEE Trans. on Pattern Analysis and Machine Intelligence*, 22(11):1330–1334. DOI: 10.1109/34.888718 Cited on page(s) 54

Zhao, J., Cheung, S. C., and Nguyen, T. (2008). Optimal camera network configurations for visual tagging. *IEEE Journal on Selected Topics in Signal Processing Special Issue on Distributed Processing in Vision Networks*. DOI: 10.1109/JSTSP.2008.2001430 Cited on page(s) 4, 5, 77

Zou, X., Bhanu, B., and Roy-Chowdhury, A. K. (2009). Continuous learning of a multilayered network topology in a video camera network. *EURASIP Journal on Image and Video Processing, Special Issue on Video-Based Modeling, Analysis, and Recognition of Human Motion*. DOI: 10.1155/2009/460689 Cited on page(s) 2, 28

Authors' Biographies

AMIT K. ROY-CHOWDHURY

Amit K. Roy-Chowdhury is an Associate Professor of Electrical Engineering and Cooperating Faculty in Computer Science at the University of California, Riverside. He received his PhD from the University of Maryland, College Park, in 2002. His research and teaching interests are in signal and image processing, computer vision and pattern recognition. He has been a Principal Investigator on a number of research projects related to motion analysis in video, camera networks and image analysis for biological applications, and has published over 100 technical articles on these topics. More information about his work can be found at `http://www.ee.ucr.edu/~amitrc/`.

BI SONG

Bi Song is Sr. Applied Research Engineer at Sony Electronics Inc, San Jose, California. She received her PhD in Electrical Engineering from the University of California, Riverside, in 2009. Her research focus has been on scene analysis in distributed camera networks and motion analysis in video. She has published more than 20 technical papers and book chapters on these topics.

Printed in the United States
by Baker & Taylor Publisher Services